THE
Woman's Day
BOOK OF
Beauty, Health
and Fitness Hints

THE
Woman's Day
BOOK OF
Beauty, Health and Fitness Hints

by Sharon Gold

Illustrated by Marika Hahn

WILLIAM MORROW AND COMPANY, INC.
NEW YORK   1980

Library of Congress Cataloging in Publication Data

Gold, Sharon.
    The Woman's day book of beauty, health, and fitness hints.

    1. Women—Health and hygiene.   2. Beauty, Personal.
I. Woman's day.   II. Title.
RA778.G68   646.7′2   80-11312
ISBN 0-688-03611-2
ISBN 0-688-08611-X pbk.

Printed in the United States of America

First Edition

1   2   3   4   5   6   7   8   9   10

Book Design by Michael Mauceri

To my grandmother

MILLIE

Contents

Introduction

It's hard to keep up with American women these days. Busy, on the go, working at careers, running households, caring for families, owning businesses, active in the community, prominent in the arts and sciences, forceful in local and national government— American women are now being *heard* as well as seen.

This is a marvelously exciting time for us. There is hardly a woman alive who has not been affected by the liberating movements of a decade ago. Traditional roles have altered—radically for some, more subtly for the majority—but one thing is sure: the life of a woman today holds more possibilities than ever before in history.

Because we are more active, fitness counts a great deal. Health is truly our most valuable possession. No longer are we dieting to fit into a dress for Sister's wedding. Now we diet because fat saps our needed energies. We diet because statistics show slimmer women are promoted more rapidly than the obese.

As we continue to hold the public eye, attractiveness counts more, too. Those first impressions do make a difference, whether at a job interview or renting an apartment. Also, there is a new sense of pride in keeping ourselves looking good. It is not simply vanity,

9

which is often empty below the surface. Rather, it is a healthy pride in our bodies. Scratch this surface, and you'll find the same healthy pride in ourselves as whole human beings.

It is to this individual that *Woman's Day* has always spoken, as friend and helper: the strong, active, involved woman who is the backbone of American life.

This book of beauty and fitness hints is also geared to that woman—to you. Within these pages, you will find over a thousand hints, tips and ideas to make beauty and fitness easier and more accessible. We know that time is a precious commodity to you, so there are no long-winded sentences, no puffed-up prose. Just quick, useful ideas you can put to work immediately within your own busy schedule.

Read straight through if you like. You'll be able to pick up all the tips that pertain to you. But you needn't start at Chapter One. You can keep this book on your bedtable and leaf through it at your leisure. Or, if you have a particular problem—your hair, for instance—you might begin with "Here's to Your Hair!" for specific advice. The chapter titles are self-explanatory, covering everything from basic skin care to travel tips. You'll find lots of miscellaneous tidbits in "Beauty Potpourri."

We hope you enjoy these hints and find many that hit the spot. We hope, too, that they give you hours of pleasure, for beauty and fitness ought to be fun. Remember, it is not a race for perfection, for no such thing exists. And it's not a competition to look better than other women, for such a goal is silly. Your beauty is for you to enjoy and to share with those lucky enough to know you.

THE
Woman's Day
BOOK OF
Beauty, Health and Fitness Hints

Chapter 1
Gorgeous Skin

The key to a great look is beautiful skin. When a woman's complexion is clear, her face radiates a special quality of vitality no makeup can duplicate. If your skin is less than perfect—and even if you've never had terrific skin—you should know that persistence and proper care will bring improvements. Follow these hints for a prettier complexion.

Identify your skin type so you can buy the correct skin care products. Wash with soap. After two hours, press your forehead, nose, chin and cheeks with a single-ply tissue. If oily spots appear, your skin's oily. It's normal if there is a little oil. If there's none, your complexion is dry.

Get into the salad habit. Eating a fresh toss of leafy greens and garden vegetables every day will provide the important vitamins and minerals that create a lively-looking complexion.

Keep cotton balls on hand for removing eye makeup and applying astringent to your skin. Bathroom tissue, made from wood pulp, is frequently harsh.

Make it a special point to cleanse and rinse with

warm water, not hot. Hot water can cause ruptured
facial capillaries—those spidery red lines that appear
around the nose and on the cheeks.

To avoid undue stretching of the skin, use circular
fingertip movements when you wash your face. Circle
over the chin, then go out along the jawline to your
ears, then across your nose to the cheekbones, then
over the nostrils, then from your eyebrows up to the
hairline. Finally, wash your neck.

If your skin has become dry, scaly or irritated for
no apparent reason, the culprit could be soap or
cleanser you've failed to wash off. Remove every last
trace by splashing your skin twenty times with plain
water after cleansing. Count each of the twenty rinses
out loud.

Baby oil makes perfect eye makeup remover. With
a clean cotton puff, swab the oil over your closed eyes.
Use a second puff and even a third if you need to—
there should be no makeup color on the last puff.

To be sure you're getting your entire face clean,
secure all your hair back off your face when you wash.
For convenience, you might keep a plastic headband
on a bathroom hook. Or store a cotton head scarf in
the vanity drawer for drawing your hair back.

Buy a soft-bristled nail brush to use as a complexion

brush. It's cheaper than the real thing, and just as effective.

To really get your skin super-clean and remove soil that washing doesn't get to, take a deep-cleansing facial "sauna": boil a pot of water and remove it from the heat source. Apply petroleum jelly to your eyes and lips. Now drape a large towel over your head *and* the pot, and let the vapors bathe your face. Don't get closer than sixteen inches—steam can burn. Sauna for five minutes once or twice a week.

A handful of dried camomile flowers added to your facial sauna pot brings out a beautiful glow in normal skin. For oily skin, use peppermint leaves and for dry skin, use dried rosemary.

Herbal steam for troubled complexions: Add dried thyme to your bubbling sauna pot to help clear up breakouts and blackheads.

Beauty shopping list for normal skin types: gentle cleansing cream or glycerine soap, mild astringent and a water-based moisturizer.

For an old-fashioned skin-slougher use oatmeal. Whisk away dead cells and embedded dirt with ordinary oatmeal (but not the instant-cook kind). Sprinkle over a wet facecloth. Rub gently over your complexion. Caution: test on a small area of the face first, as oatmeal may irritate some sensitive skins.

In hard-water areas, use a glycerine soap. It lathers easier and cleans better than most other soaps.

Before menstruation, skin is usually oilier. At this time of the month, use astringent more frequently. You may also wish to cleanse one extra time daily.

Memorize "C.T.M." That means Cleanse, Tone and Moisturize—your three daily skin-care steps. Cleanse with a soap, cleanser or gel; tone with astringent or freshener; and moisturize with a moisturizing product. Gear all products to your skin type—and do all the steps every day.

Beauty shopping list for oily skin: low-alkaline glycerine soap or oily-skin wash, high-alcohol astringent and water-based moisturizer.

Pat your face dry with a soft terry towel—don't rub it or scrub vigorously. Remember, keep the drying process gentle on this delicate skin to avoid pulling.

Very oily skin should be cleansed three times daily. If you can't wash at midday, blot the excess oils from your complexion with a packaged face towelette.

Beauty shopping list for dry skin: rich cleansing cream or super-fatted soap, alcohol-free freshener and emollient-rich moisturizer.

Sweet-smelling almond oil makes a marvelous cleanser for sensitive skins. Pour a capful into the cup of your palm. Apply to your face with the other hand. Smooth the oil lightly over your skin, then rinse and pat dry. Almond oil is available at most health food stores.

On extra-dry skin, use soap only at night since even the mildest soap can be somewhat drying. In the morning, simply splash your face with tepid water and pat dry with a towel.

Don't use bath soap on your face. Clean your complexion with the special soap or cleanser for your skin type. Bath soap is formulated with perfumes that can irritate your face.

Ashy skin needs lots of moisturizing since it's too dry. Carry a purse-size moisturizer in your bag for "touch-ups" during the day.

Sudden skin breakouts may be caused by a new cosmetic or skin-care product. Determine if your irritation coincides with the use of a new product.

Avoiding sharp cheeses will sometimes help keep a sensitive skin under control. Try staying away from cheddar, roquefort, gorgonzola and other pungent cheeses when breakouts occur. See if this ploy helps— some dermatologists feel it does.

Squeezing blackheads is *not* recommended. But if you remove an occasional one, do it this way: first apply a hot compress to soften the skin. Soak a clean washcloth in hot water, wring it out and press over the blackhead. Repeat three times, then gently clean the pore by wrapping both your index fingers with tissue and applying gentle pressure on either side of the clogged pore. Swab afterward with astringent.

If you use an acne remedy containing retinoic acid (also called tretinoin), avoid exposing the treated area to sunlight or to a sunlamp. The drug's combination with ultraviolet rays increases the danger of skin cancer, latest research shows.

Reserve a special towel for facial use only since dirt and perspiration from other body parts may irritate the more sensitive skin of your face. Replace with a fresh towel every three days.

Scour your bathroom sink daily to keep it sparkling clean. Rinse away the cleansing powder residue so none finds its way to your complexion where its harshness can irritate.

An excellent blackhead-loosener: Mix equal parts of cleansing cream and yellow cornmeal. Mix to a paste. Use as a facial scrub, massaging into large-pore areas. Then cleanse and apply your regular astringent or witch hazel.

Milk of magnesia will dry up oily blackheads. Apply with a cotton swab and leave on overnight.

Cold sores are annoying, to be sure. You can speed their cure with over-the-counter spirits of camphor. If you are subject to chronic sores, consult a dermatologist. Though no permanent remedy is yet known, a stronger medication may be prescribed by your doctor.

To ease the itch of poison ivy, apply a compress of ice-cold milk. Saturate a clean piece of cheesecloth and press over the rash.

Think twice about self-prescribing vitamin A to clear up a poor complexion. Exceeding the recommended daily requirement of A can be unsafe for some people.

Instant night cream for dry skin: mineral oil. Smooth some on in a thin film over face and neck before you retire.

Baby cream makes a sensuous night cream for your face. And it's got that lovely, sweet smell to make you sleep like a baby, too.

Save money my mixing your own skin freshener: one part rubbing alcohol to four parts distilled water.

Witch hazel is a wonderful astringent, and very cheap. Make it seem more "feminine" by storing it in a pretty bottle of your own.

Lighten facial hair with a mixture of half hydrogen peroxide, half ammonia and enough mild soap flakes to make a paste. Leave on five minutes, then rinse off. Do a patch test first on a small spot of skin to see if you are sensitive.

Avoid nervous facial gestures, frowning, squinting and resting your cheek on your hand. Too much pulling of the skin may cause wrinkles.

Sleep on your back and you'll discourage wrinkles— you'll be sleeping crease-free.

Buy a humidifier for any room that is overheated or air-conditioned since a too-dry environment encourages further drying, scaling and wrinkling of the skin. You can set up your own humidifying system by placing a large pan of water on top of the radiator. Be sure to keep the window open a little.

Keep your chin up! It's not only good for morale but makes shadows and puffs under the eyes look less dark.

One way to keep wrinkles at bay is to apply a sunblock whenever your face is exposed to the sun's strong rays. Skin of every color will benefit from this.

Dispel upper-lip lines with this exercise: alternate puckering for a kiss and stretching your upper lip down over your upper teeth.

Nose-to-mouth lines are discouraged by puffing your cheeks out as if you were blowing up a balloon. Let the air out slowly and repeat.

Tighten a slack jawline by dropping your head back and letting your mouth fall open naturally. Now close your mouth, feeling your neck muscles do the hard work. Keep opening and closing for fifteen seconds.

Tiny hairs in your nostrils should never be tweezed. First, tweezing this sensitive spot is very painful, and second, tweezing risks ingrown hairs and infection. Instead, snip the visible hairs with a sterilized cuticle scissors.

Face cream is too rich to waste. Any cream left over on your fingers should be rubbed into knees, elbows, heels—whatever places are rough or dry.

If your hair is oily, keep your hair squeaky clean with frequent shampooing—daily, if necessary—to prevent greasy hair from irritating your complexion.

If you have combination skin—part oily and part dry—wash the dry area with a rich cleanser and the oily area with a low-alkaline cleanser to stabilize both parts.

Hard water makes it difficult to remove soap residue from your skin after cleansing. If you live in a hard-water area, use distilled water from a bottle for rinsing, and not tap water.

Petroleum jelly is an inexpensive moisturizer. But be sure you spread it on very, very thinly over a damp face to avoid a greasy look and feel.

No matter how late you get in at night, take a few minutes to wash your face. Don't fall into bed with makeup clogging your pores.

Keep your hands away from your face! Our hands are in contact with more bacteria than any other part of our bodies. To avoid irritating your skin, break the bad habit of fiddling with your face.

Don't forget to apply moisturizer to your throat as well as your face. It's there that the skin is delicate, with few oil glands to provide natural lubrication.

Gardeners should wear a loose cotton scarf or man's handkerchief around their necks when working. Exposing your neck to the sun when you weed promotes dry skin and wrinkling.

Cut down on alcohol and cigarettes to avoid wrinkles. Too much liquor dehydrates the skin, and continually pursing the lips while smoking causes aging lines.

Chapter 2

That Fabulous Face

With a healthy complexion, you can begin the fun of making up your face—like an artist begins to paint a portrait on fresh canvas. Foundation, concealer, blusher—these cosmetics lay the basis for the creative coloring that comes later on. Though more subtle than either eyes or lips, your skin makeup is very important. Spend time choosing the correct products, and learn to perfect these fundamental steps.

Zoom in on your nose, your eyebrows and your entire face with a magnifying mirror. Using one is the best way to perfect your makeup techniques.

For a super-smooth face look, always moisturize before you apply foundation. Gently smooth moisturizer over your entire face, including your lips.

Shopping for foundation? Test various shades on your neck, and you're sure to end up with a color that seems natural and doesn't look like a mask.

Can't decide what your skin color is? Remove all your makeup, wrap a white towel around your head and put on a white blouse or tee shirt. Stand in natural light—outdoors or at a window—and look in a mirror.

Without the distractions of hair and clothing color, you'll more easily know if you are ivory, peach, ruddy, olive, tan, brown or brown-black. If you still can't make up your mind, ask two friends for their opinions.

If you have great skin—healthy and even-toned, without any discolorations—you need not cover your face with foundation. Just wear base over your nose, cheeks and chin, in the center of your face: then powder lightly for a finished matte look.

As you get older, wear less foundation, not more. A thick layer of base quickly settles into lines and wrinkles, making them very obvious.

Invest in a good foundation to give you perfect color and coverage for a healthy and vital look. A foundation that spreads evenly, has a scent that appeals to you and covers facial imperfections is the one for you.

Thin out a too-heavy, water-based foundation with water. In the palm of your hand, blend the base with just one or two drops of water, then apply as usual. An oil-based foundation can be made sheerer by adding one or two drops of moisturizer. Follow the same steps as for water-based foundation.

A face with lots of fine hair looks better in a moisturized makeup, and not matte. Be sure to stroke it on in the direction in which the hairs grow, and not against the growth, to make them less noticeable.

Adolescent acne? Choose a medicated, water-based makeup or daytime cover without any oils. Acne is frequently associated with oversized, overactive pores. The last thing you need is more oil to clog them further!

To camouflage tiny acne scars, dot concealing stick or cream over them with a pointed brush. Then apply your foundation.

The undereye area is delicate, so apply creams or makeup with a patting motion of the fingertip. Don't stretch the skin.

An extra-rich foundation can be homemade by mixing a tiny bit of night cream with your regular base. Blend them in the palm of your hand, then apply.

For very oily skin that shines no matter what you do, mix a few drops of astringent in with your regular base. The astringent will help blot those oils. Blend in the palm of your hand.

Do you want to hide those lines and wrinkles? Draw over them with a concealing stick one shade lighter than your base. Blend the lines with your finger. Now stroke on your foundation.

If your eyes are too close together, you can make

them seem farther apart by dotting light concealer in the inside corners of your eyes and over the bridge of your nose. Blend the cream in well.

A low, low forehead will appear higher if you smooth foundation one shade lighter than your normal color just below the hairline. Blend it well with your regular base.

Apply your foundation the professional way for super-smooth results: Use a damp makeup sponge to blend your base over your complexion. Rinse the sponge clean after each use.

Is your face too long? Apply foundation one shade darker than your regular color on your forehead, and it will look shorter.

A chin that's weak or recedes can be brought forward by covering it with foundation a shade lighter than your regular base. Blend the light color under your chin, too.

A jutting chin can seem overpowering. To soften it, blend a darker shade of foundation over it. Take the darker color under the chin, and use your fingertips to blend for naturalness. Check that there are no demarcation lines.

Flesh out a thin, pointy nose by smoothing lighter

foundation over the sides and nostrils and darker foundation over the tip.

For a nose that's too long, cover the tip and nostrils with foundation one shade darker than your regular base.

Give a shapeless nose more definition: Stroke dark foundation along either side of it. Now apply a thin line of highlighter down the center. Blend all colors.

Sunken cheeks can be filled out by stroking a lighter foundation in the hollows.

Color scheme for an ivory complexion: ivory or pale beige foundation and light, translucent face powder. In blusher, choose the soft reds, roses or peaches.

Flatter your peaches-and-cream skin with a peachy-beige foundation and a light face powder. Wear a soft red, red-brown or bronze blusher.

For olive skin, wear a light or medium beige base and medium face powder. Choose blusher in the true red, rosy-red or rosy-peach families.

Play down your ruddy skin tones with a medium beige foundation and medium translucent face powder. Opt for blusher in the brown, bronze or earthy-red families.

Match your own tan skin tones with a beige-tan or suntan foundation and medium powder. Very appealing on you are blushers in the red, deep rose and red-brown ranges.

Lustrous brown skin should wear medium brown, mocha or sepia base and deep translucent powder. Blushers look great on you in plum, earth-red or rust.

Best colors for a dark brown-black skin: deep brown, umber or sable foundation and dark translucent face powder. In blusher, go with plums, brown-reds, deep rust.

How about using an "undertoner" to correct your complexion color subtly? These are bases that go under your foundation and come in lavender to play up a pale skin, pale green to tone down a ruddy skin and apricot to warm up a sallow skin.

Use an apricot undertoner to offset the yellow and graying look of a faded suntan.

If your foundation turns yellow, switch to a beige shade and stay away from the peachy colors.

For a bright and lively look, dot highlighter on the

places the sun reflects—the middle of your forehead, the ridge of your nose, your chin. You'll look sun-kissed. (Highlighter is a white or pearlized cream sold by most cosmetic makers.)

Give a small face the illusion of width by blending highlighter at your temples and along the jawline.

How about a man's shaving brush for dusting on your loose face powder! Be sure it's one of the super-soft types that feels furry to the touch.

Need a great nighttime face powder? You can use either baby powder or cornstarch. Buff them on with a fresh cotton puff.

Whisk excess face powder away with a clean cotton ball or cosmetic puff.

Save small spice bottles for blending your own cus-tom-made foundation shades. Sterilize the jars before using.

To get the most natural blusher look, blend the line where your foundation and blusher meet. Use your fingertips to soften the line so it's invisible.

Where should you apply blusher? On the apples of your cheeks. When you smile, those are the plump circles you see. Use an upward, diagonal stroke to take the blusher out to your temples.

You can soften the angles of a square face by applying your blusher at the tops of the cheeks and blending up along the highest part of the cheekbones. Don't take the blusher all the way out to your temples.

A face that's overly long can't take too much color in the center—it crowds the area that should look most open. Concentrate blusher at the outer cheeks and temples.

Get both cheeks even when you blush. Apply fresh blusher to your brush for each cheek. If you're using a cream blusher, dip your finger into the pot twice— once for each cheek.

On days when you look tired, dust blusher over your forehead, chin and nose as well as on your cheeks. That faint rosy glow, like a slight sunburn, will make you look less worn-out.

Dab a little blusher on your earlobe—it's an alluring evening trick, especially if you're wearing tiny earrings or none at all.

If you're touching up your blusher during the day and you know you'll be putting it on over face powder, carry a powder blush compact. Cream blush will smear your powder.

If you've been too generous with your blusher, you can soften the color by dusting over your cheeks with sheer face powder.

Do you like a high-fashion look in makeup? Try brushing brown contour shading along the hollows under your cheekbones. The effect is quite dramatic, and strictly for evening wear.

With scissors, cut open used-up foundation and blusher tubes. You'll be surprised at how many extra applications you'll get from what's left in there.

You can substitute artists' brushes for expensive makeup brushes. Art brushes are made of the finest materials and are sometimes cheaper than cosmetic brushes. Check an art supply store for prices.

Chapter 3

The Eyes Have It!

*Like glimmering jewels, eyes are the important as-
set of every woman's face. No eyes are unappealing;
every eye is lovely. All it takes is a bit of expertise to
play up their importance. Do take the time to shape
your brows, the eyes' natural frame. Eyebrows can
often do more than makeup to enhance, but they must
never overwhelm. Your mascara can give you a wide-
eyed beauty. Care for your eyes and keep them healthy
with exercise and the proper glasses, if necessary—
and your "gems" will keep their special luster always.*

Save the cash you now spend on special eye makeup
remover by substituting vegetable oil or petroleum
jelly.

If you wake up with puffy eyelids, wait a while before applying your makeup. Cotton balls soaked in
ice water and pressed gently over your lids will help
ease the puffiness, which is usually caused by retained
fluids.

For eyelids that are darker than your complexion
or discolored, use a special eye makeup base or concealing stick. Smooth the lighter color over your eyelids, then put on makeup.

Create your own "private collection" eyeshadows by combining shades you have. For example, blue plus brown makes smoky blue. White plus any color makes a lighter shade of that color which you can use to highlight. Layer the colors right on your eyelid, or combine them in the palm of your hand, then apply.

A great model's trick: Smooth a neutral color like taupe or khaki from the lashline right up to the browbone. Blend well. Line your eyes with a coordinating color (brown or forest green, in this case) and finish with two coats of black mascara.

Use blue eyeliner pencil on your bottom eyelids for a bright-eyed look. Blue makes the whites of your eyes appear whiter. Just use care when penciling the inner lid above the base of the lashes.

Narrow eyeliner makes eyes look bigger. Heavy eyeliner, drawn on in a thicker line, makes them look smaller.

To enlarge tiny eyes, apply bright blue or green eyeliner from the center of your eye out to the corner.

A soft eye look is pretty. Smudge your liner with a cotton swab for a subtle makeup that goes beautifully with delicate fashions.

Accent eye makeup *under* your eyes if you wear

bangs or brow waves. Bring your shadow around and under and line the lower lid.

Give eyes sparkle with a dot of gleaming highlighter just above the pupil, right over your shadow. This is a great nighttime trick.

Are your eyelids oily? Before you put on mascara, go over your eyeshadow lightly with translucent powder. Apply it with a cotton puff. This way, the color won't settle in your eye creases and your makeup will look fresh for hours.

Never, never use white concealing cream around your eyes. You'll look like a raccoon!

Spark your blue eyes with brown, gray, plum, olive or violet eyeshadow colors.

Super shadow for green eyes: teal blue, forest green, gray, plum and mauve.

Hazel eyes look wonderful in bronze, teal blue, deep green, navy and gold.

Your gray eyes can wear many colors—khaki, plum, ivy green, Prussian blue and cocoa are a few of them.

Colors for brown eyes? Brown, plum, navy, forest green and taupe.

Black eyes love intense colors as well as the more subtle ones. Try charcoal, bronze, berry, teal, mint green, aqua and gold.

Use kids' crayons to try out new eyeshadow colors without spending a penny. Here's how: Get a clean sheet of paper. Over it, draw as many eyes as you can fit—just a simple shape with a lid. Now study your own eyes in the mirror. Use crayons to duplicate the color (you may have to mix a few colors to get your exact shade). Fill in every eye on the paper in your color. Now test out "eye shadows." Use different crayons and blends of colors to see how they work with your eye color. Try everything—even pinks, mauves and yellows. When you find colors you like, take your paper to the store and try to match the shadow colors in makeup.

On wide-set eyes, use darker shadow between the inner corner of the eye and the bridge of the nose to give the appearance of closer proportion.

You want to minimize a prominent or bulgy eyelid? Stick to darker, muted shadow like brown, navy or smoky gray that plays down the lid instead of emphasizing it, as a light color would do.

If you've got small eyes, stay away from the dark shadows. They'll make your eyes look even tinier.

Wear lighter shades like pink, yellow and other pastel eye shadows.

Close-set eyes are "widened" with lighter shadow applied between the inner eye corner and the midpoint of the lid. Use a darker shade from the midpoint to the outer corner. Mascara should go on the outer lashes only.

A droopy or overhanging brow can be minimized with a medium or smoky shade stroked over the entire brow, from the crease line of the eye up to the eyebrow itself.

If your eyes droop down at the corners, give them a lift by applying all your eye makeup with upward strokes. Your shadow should go up at the corners in a "V."

If you've got a pointy chin, draw attention away from it by lifting your eyeshadow up at the corners, out toward the temples.

Give depth to your eye with a dark shadow in the crease of the lid. Use brown, charcoal or any deep shade. Stroke it in the hollow, along the crease (you can feel it with your finger above the eyeball). Blend the color well. This is a terrific nighttime trick.

Dark, bold eyebrows call for striking eye makeup.

Wear intense colors and be sure to balance your dominant brows with a bright lipstick.

It's dull to match shadow to your eye color. Wear a complementary shade.

To widen your eyes, use an eyelash curler. Before you mascara, gently press the curler at the lash base and count to ten.

Give your lashes a long look: Apply the first coat to the top side of your upper lashes. When it's dry, roll the second coat on the underside, as you usually do.

Wear black mascara at night. Black intensifies your eyes, adds wonderful drama. Whatever color you wear during the day, mascara should be black on your evening lashes.

Wear a colored mascara. Blue and green eyes look more intense in navy; gray eyes look bluer or greener depending on whether you put on dark blue or dark green; and brown eyes seem deeper in a wine or burgundy mascara.

Eliminate mascara smudges by protecting the skin under your bottom lashes with a cotton swab.

Create thick-looking lashes by dusting loose powder over your first coat of mascara. Use your index finger. Then apply the second coat.

Prevent eye infections by replacing your mascara every few months.

Trim your false eyelashes with a cuticle scissors. Cut them shorter at the inner corner. Then thin them in general so they look natural.

Tweeze stray brow hairs every other day. If you keep up with them, it's easy to maintain the line. And your brows will always be well-groomed.

Want to see how you look in a different eyebrow shape? "Remove" your old brows with concealer— just stroke it over the hairs so they're covered completely. Now pencil in the new line to see how it looks. If you stand back where you can't see the details, you'll get a pretty good idea. Repeat this process until you find your most flattering shape.

Tweeze s-l-o-w-l-y. Pluck one hair at a time, then inspect. Try to match both your brows so they look like a pair.

Tweeze your brows from the inside corner and work your way out.

Before using, sterilize your tweezers in boiling

water. You can also swab them with alcohol to clean
them.

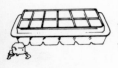

Tweezing needn't hurt. Press an ice cube over your
brow area to anesthetize the skin, and the whole thing
will be practically painless.

If your eyes are too close, pluck a few extra hairs
at the inside corner (the beginning of the brow). This
will have the effect of "separating" your eyes.

With eyes too far apart, tweeze a few extra hairs at
the end of the brow. Shortening your eyebrow will
seem to draw your eyes closer together.

Minimize the arch to shorten an oblong face. You'll
look better in a straighter brow.

Accent the eyebrow arch to make a round face
seem less so.

Eyebrows too low? Tweeze from underneath until
your eyes look clear and wide-awake.

If your hair is light and your coloring light and
your eyebrows very dark, you may want to lighten
them so they don't overwhelm your face. Have your
beautician do this job.

Instant brow lightener: Rub a little foundation into your brow hairs, then brush into place. A good alternative is face powder, again brushed into the brows.

To avoid a harsh, artificial look, draw eyebrow pencil on in tiny, feathery lines that look exactly like your own brow hairs. Pencil them in the same direction as your own hairs. Brush with a soft toothbrush for a natural effect.

To give your brows a pretty shine, go over them with an eyebrow brush to remove excess makeup, then gloss them lightly with petroleum jelly.

A glamorous eye trick models use is to brush your brows up with a toothbrush, then rub clear glycerine soap over them in an upward direction to keep that feathered look in place.

Tame unruly brows with clear moustache wax. Or spray hairspray on an extra toothbrush and brush those eyebrows into place.

Two damp, cool tea bags placed over your eyelids will act quickly to soothe tired eyes.

Perk up exhausted eyes by saturating cotton balls with ice water. Relax for ten minutes with the pads resting on your eyelids.

Eyes need exercise, like any other muscle of the body. Keep your head still as you look all the way up, then to the right, and down, and finally to the left. Reverse the direction and repeat.

When shopping for new eyeglasses, try on each pair of frames before a full-length mirror. In a small mirror, you won't get a sense of proportion—if the glasses are the right size for you in relation to your figure.

Nearsighted women should exaggerate eye makeup a bit—your eyeglass lenses make your eyes look smaller than they actually are.

If you're farsighted, wear soft rather than dramatic eye makeup, since lenses tend to enlarge your eyes a little. Avoid very bright colors, and keep the application subtle.

Use a soft toothbrush and a gentle detergent to scrub the crevices of your eyeglasses from time to time.

Rectangular or geometric frames add interesting facial angles to a very round face.

Soften your square face with curved frames— round, large oval or anything *not* square and angular.

Is your face oblong? Deep, rectangular eyeglass frames that cover part of your cheeks will give you a better-balanced look.

Good choices for a heart-shaped face with a narrow chin are pretty ovals or small rectangles. Choose a neat, balanced frame—nothing that overwhelms your delicate face shape.

A low bridge on your glasses will shorten your nose if it's too long.

Pick glasses with a high bridge if you want your nose to look longer.

A clear bridge with darker sides will widen close-set eyes by drawing attention outward.

Soft contact lens wearers should insert their lenses before making up their eyes. Putting them in after makes it easy for specks of makeup to get stuck to those delicate lenses.

If you wear contact lenses, use cream eyeshadows, don't line inside your eyelids and avoid "lash-building" mascaras.

Dark green and gray sunglasses offer most protection to the eyes.

Consider wearing protective plastic goggles if you are doing carpentry, spray-painting outdoors where the wind can blow or refinishing furniture—any work that produces flying matter.

Do you have wrinkles around your eyes? When you buy new eyeglasses, have the lens tinted slightly. The faint color won't interfere with your vision, but it will help to camouflage your lines and crow's feet.

Chapter 4

Your Marvelous Mouth

Your mouth lets you express yourself to the world. It is the instrument of many of life's great pleasures— talking, laughing, kissing, eating, singing. . . . Naturally your mouth gets a large share of attention. You'll want it to appear soft, smooth and appealing. Keep your teeth sparkling, your breath sweet and your lips attractively colored with some of these easy-to-follow ideas:

Calm shaky hands when applying lipstick. Rest your elbow on a table, and steady your chin on your bent-in pinky.

If you're feeling extravagant, buy two or three different lipbrushes, one for each lipstick you use regularly.

You can chip your teeth if you open clips, curlers or bobby pins with your mouth. Don't use your teeth for breaking thread or opening bottles, either.

If you're using lip wax on your upper lip, remove it quickly against the direction of the hair growth for the smoothest waxing results.

Lipstick and nail polish don't have to match exactly, but they should be in the same color family—red with red, rosy-reds with rose or pink, and orange-red with orange, coral or rust.

If your mouth droops down at the corners, tilt your lipliner up slightly at the corners—not so much that it looks fake, but just enough to make your expression brighter. Apply color more intensely at the center of your lips to keep the emphasis there.

For a too-thin top lip, line slightly outside your natural lipline on top. Fill in with color. If you use a slightly lighter lipstick shade on the top lip, it will look even fuller.

Create a pretty bow in a straight-across top lip. With lip pencil, lightly mark two dots directly under each nostril on your top lipline. Between the dots draw a rounded "V." Line the rest of your mouth following your natural liplines and fill in with lipstick.

Lips that are two different colors can be evened out by stroking light cover-up cream on the darker lip only. Powder it afterwards, then apply your lipstick as usual.

Tip for crooked lips: Even out the left and right sides of a lopsided mouth by making both lips match with lipliner. Copy the better side. Then apply lip-color in the lines.

To accentuate skinny lips: First, cover your lips with concealing cream, then line slightly outside your natural lipline with a lip pencil a shade darker than your lipstick. Fill in with the lipstick and top with clear gloss. That shine will make your mouth look fuller.

Slim too-full lips by drawing an outline slightly— very slightly—inside your natural lipline. Fill in with the identical color lipstick. Choose subtle colors that won't bring extra attention to your mouth, and stay away from frosteds and lip gloss.

It's socially acceptable to refresh your lipstick in a restaurant or other public place, but save a complete makeup redo for the rest room.

Running an ice cube over your freshly applied lipstick will set the color so it keeps for hours.

Does your lipstick always go out of your liplines? Lick the problem by first dusting your lips with translucent powder to dry up any oils. Then outline with lipliner pencil—its waxy ingredients act as a barrier to lipstick, which is much oilier. And finally, apply your lipstick with a lipbrush for the most control. If you like a matte effect, you can powder your lips again lightly.

Lipcolors for ivory skin: true red, medium rose and peach. Avoid brown and earth-red.

For olive skin, go with clear red, deep rose, peach or coral. Stay away from orange-brown.

Earth-reds, true reds and dark rose shades are best-bet shades for tan skin. No orangy colors.

Flatter a peachy complexion with lipstick in soft red, amber and red-brown. Don't wear pink or yellow-orange tones.

Advice for brown skins—lipsticks look good on you in true red, copper, red-brown and brown. Avoid frosteds.

Ruddy faces need to be toned down with pretty earth shades, ambers and brown lipsticks. Hot reds and pinks just aren't for you.

Dark brown complexions look marvelous in deep plums, wines, earthy reds and dark browns. Don't use light colors or frosteds.

A dot of gold powder or gold stick makeup right smack in the center of your lower lip is a dazzling evening lip tip.

If you have gorgeous, super-white teeth, show them off with sizzling red and rosy-pink lipstick colors.

A "beauty mark" dotted by the corner of your mouth can be alluring. Use brown eyebrow pencil, and press the dot with your finger so it looks real. Practice this one before the night of the party!

Outline the bow of your upper lip with a bit of pearlized highlighter for a dewy party look.

Use the flat end of a toothpick dipped in skin cleanser to fix lipstick smudges. Gently remove the smear.

Mature women look terrific in clear red, or a subtle, deep rose lipstick. Don't wear anything very light, very dark or orangy.

Don't use toothpicks to pick your teeth—they can cause receding gums. Brush after every meal instead. If you're away from home at midday, carry a purse-size toothbrushing kit with a fold-up toothbrush and mini toothpaste!

Are you a sports fanatic? Automatically put on lip moisturizer with sunscreen if you're competing out-doors.

Be an artist! Invent great new lip shades by wearing different lip glosses over your lipstick. Real red gloss over rose lipstick makes a deep rose color. How about copper gloss over red lipstick for a brick color?

The cheapest lip gloss: petroleum jelly.

Feeling down in the dumps? Retouching your lipstick will give you an instant lift. Try it and see.

Don't discard broken lipsticks. You can fix them by heating the broken ends over a candle and pressing them together. Then cool the lipstick in the refrigerator.

Keep your lipsticks from drying out—cap them tightly.

A boring old lipstick will suddenly take on new zing if you apply it over a second shade to create a fresh color.

One way to banish bad breath: Have your teeth cleaned by your dentist every six months—more often, if you have gum problems. Let your dentist advise you.

Brush your teeth up and down, in the direction they grow: brush down on your upper teeth and up on your lower teeth.

Unwaxed dental floss is best for cleaning under the gum line, since waxy floss may leave a residue.

Don't scour your teeth excessively to get them white. Not all teeth are white-white naturally. A yellowish cast is normal and doesn't indicate ill health.

Use "disclosing tablets" every night for three weeks to perfect your toothbrushing technique. These tablets temporarily stain any plaque on your teeth a dark pink color. You brush to remove it and get to know which areas you need to brush better. Disclosing tablets are sold at drugstores.

Parsley is a natural breath freshener. Don't discard that sprightly bit of green on your fish or potato—chew it to erase garlic or onion odors.

Don't give mouth wrinkles any encouragement. Everyday, lubricate all around your lips with moisturizer.

Some women clench their teeth and set their mouths tightly, usually due to nerves. Try to become aware when you are doing this—and stop! Continued tension around the mouth contributes to wrinkling.

Replace your toothbrush about every two months. After this time, the bristles usually lose their shape and can't do an effective cleaning job.

Don't stock up on too much fluoride toothpaste. After about six months the fluoride will start to lose its potency. So take advantage of sales and specials, but buy only what you'll use within a half year.

Chapter 5

Home Beauty Treatments

With the hundreds of beauty care items crowding our drugstore shelves, you'd hardly think it necessary for any woman to spend time preparing her own products from scratch. If it isn't exactly a need, sometimes cooking up skin cleansers, face packs and hair conditioners from kitchen ingredients is plain fun. After all, our grandmothers used many of the identical recipes! Home beauty treatments are also great money-savers for a tight budget. Use good sense with homemade products. If you are allergic to a particular ingredient—strawberries or tomatoes, for example—as a food, you're likely to show sensitivity when it's applied topically to your skin. Test all treatments on a small patch of skin before using over a larger area.

Orange Cleanser (to cleanse oily skin): Over a low flame, heat 1 tablespoon fresh-squeezed orange juice. Remove from heat and mix in ¼ teaspoon borax. In a separate pot, melt 6 tablespoons petroleum jelly. Beat juice-borax mixture into jelly until consistency is creamy. To use, massage the cleanser over your face and neck. Remove with warm water and a washcloth. Refrigerate between uses.

New England Astringent (to cleanse and tone oily skin): Combine 1 ounce apple cider vinegar and 1 ounce distilled water. Apply with a cotton ball to your face and neck. If you see dirt on the cotton, repeat with a fresh piece of cotton. Repeat until cotton is soil-free. Refrigerate between uses.

Almond-plus Mask (to deep-cleanse oily skin): Combine the white of 1 egg, 1 tablespoon pulverized almonds and a squeeze of fresh lemon in a glass or ceramic bowl. Use immediately. Apply over face, except for the eye area and mouth, with fingertips. Leave on 20 minutes, then rinse with warm water. Splash cool water over face.

Quick Health Mask (to deep-cleanse oily skin): Mix 2 tablespoons brewer's yeast with 2 tablespoons skim milk to form a paste. Spread over your skin and rinse off with warm water after 10 minutes.

Buttermilk Mask (to tighten oily skin): Add enough buttermilk to dry oatmeal to form a thick paste. Apply immediately to your skin. Leave on 20 minutes, then rinse off with warm water.

Rich-Girl Cleanser (to cleanse dry skin): Mix a few drops of your favorite cologne in a bottle of vegetable oil. To cleanse, massage over your complexion with your fingertips and tissue off. Refrigerate between uses.

Grandmother's Freshener (to tone dry skin): Shake ¼ cup glycerine with 1 cup rose water together in a bottle. Apply with a cotton puff over your face and neck.

California Health Mask (to moisturize and deep-cleanse dry skin): Blend ½ ripe avocado until smooth. Place in the top of a double boiler and heat the avocado until warm. Apply over your face—except for the eyes and mouth—and rinse off after 15 minutes with splashes of warm water.

Honey-plus Mask (to soften and deep-cleanse dry skin): Whip 1 egg and mix 1 tablespoon honey into it. With your fingertips, apply all over your face. Leave on for 20 minutes, then take off with warm water. Follow with a cool rinse.

Banana Mask (to lubricate and cleanse dry skin): Blend 1 medium or large banana until creamy smooth. Apply over your skin, avoiding the eyes and mouth. After 15 minutes, rinse with clear warm water.

Wake-up Cleanser (to cleanse normal skin): Mix 2 tablespoons strained, fresh-squeezed lemon juice into 6 tablespoons vegetable shortening. Beat until smooth. Apply to your skin with your fingertips. Refrigerate between uses.

Almond Freshener (to cleanse and tone normal skin): Shake together in a bottle 3 ounces almond extract, 2 ounces witch hazel and ⅛ teaspoon alum. Stroke over your skin after cleansing, using a cotton ball. Refrigerate between uses.

Cucumber Freshener (to tone normal skin): Peel

1 cucumber and place in a blender with 3 ounces water. Blend for 2 minutes. Pat over your skin with cotton balls. Refrigerate between uses.

All-Milk Mask (to deep-cleanse normal skin): Mix enough buttermilk with dry milk powder to make a thick paste. Apply to your skin immediately, except for the eye area and your mouth. Leave on for 20 minutes, then rinse off with warm water. Follow with a cool-water rinse.

Grapefruit-Protein Mask (to nourish and tone normal skin): Add enough fresh-squeezed, strained grapefruit juice to protein powder (available in health food stores) to form a smooth paste. Apply with fingertips to your skin. After 10 minutes, rinse off with warm water.

Blemish Lotion (to cleanse and tone troubled skin): Mix together 1 ounce powdered alum, 1 ounce lemon juice and 1 pint rose water. Bottle and refrigerate. To use, shake and saturate a cotton puff with the lotion. Swab gently over your skin. Note: You may use this lotion on your back as well as your face.

Camphor Mask (to deep-cleanse and release excess oils in troubled skin): Beat the white of 1 egg slightly. Mix into it 1 teaspoon camphorated oil. Apply to your skin with your fingers. Leave on 20 minutes and rinse off with warm water, followed by splashes of cool water.

Almond Moisturizer (to moisturize and soften the complexion): Combine 1 tablespoon witch hazel, 2 tablespoons glycerine, 5 tablespoons distilled water and 2 drops almond extract. Bottle in a pretty container. After cleansing and toning, apply to your complexion using your fingertips.

Bran-Yogurt Mask (to deep-cleanse troubled skin): Blend 4 tablespoons bran until fine. Add enough plain yogurt to form a thick paste. Pat onto skin and leave on for 15 minutes. To remove, rinse with warm water.

Rosemary-Mint Mouthwash (to sweeten the breath): Steep 1 teaspoon dried peppermint leaves and 1 teaspoon dried rosemary in 2 pints boiling water. Strain and store in a bottle in the refrigerator. Use full-strength as you would any regular mouthwash.

Old-fashioned Eye Cream (to moisturize and nourish the eye area): Over a low flame, melt together 1 teaspoon beeswax, 1 teaspoon heavy mineral oil and ½ teaspoon anhydrous lanolin. Beat until cool. Store in a cosmetic jar. To use, apply gently with fingertips around eye area.

Flower Garden Body Oil (to moisturize and soften your skin): Pick (or buy) fragrant rose blossoms, gardenias, magnolias or your own favorite sweet-smelling flower. Fill a pottery jar to the top with the petals. Pour in a bit of olive oil. Cover the jar and store for one month in a cool, dark spot—like a closet. Then strain out the oil and use it by rubbing it over your body.

Easy Massage Oil (for massages or as a body oil): Melt 1¼ tablespoons lanolin in the top of a double boiler. In another pot, warm 1 cup vegetable oil. Remove both from the heat and mix together. Store in a bottle. To use, take a little in the palms of your hands and smooth over your body. For a massage, warm the oil over a low heat.

Best Bath Oil (to lubricate the skin): Mix 1 cup safflower oil with 2 teaspoons fragrant shampoo in a blender. Bottle. For each bath, pour a capful under the running faucet.

Castile Bubble Bath (as a bath cleanser and just for fun, too!): Buy a block of pure castile soap or use your favorite bath bar. With a fine grater, make tiny soap shavings. Keep them in a jar. Add a handful to your bath water.

Good Mud Bath (to deep-cleanse and stimulate circulation): Buy a bag of sterilized potting soil. Sprinkle into a large baking pan (or two). Bake in a 450° oven for 20 minutes. Remove and cool. Mix with distilled water until pasty. Pat the mud all over your face and body. Let it dry for 5–10 minutes until caky. Wash off in a warm shower. Follow with a cool shower to close your pores.

Cleopatra Bath (for smooth, soft skin): Pour 1 package or 1 cup dry powdered milk under running bath water, and step in!

Rosemary Shampoo (to bring out the highlights in dark hair): Steep 6 heaping teaspoons rosemary in 1 quart boiled water for 3 hours. Strain. Heat 2 ounces castile soap in top of a double boiler. Dissolve in the rosemary water and bottle for use. Apply as you would any shampoo.

Camomile Shampoo (to bring out the highlights in blond or light brown hair: In the preceding recipe, substitute 6 heaping teaspoons camomile flowers for the rosemary. Then follow the identical directions.

Oily Hair Shampoo (to shampoo oily hair): To either of the two preceding recipes, add 3 ounces witch hazel.

Yogurt Hair Conditioner (to bring out the shine in and restore condition to dry or damaged hair): After shampooing and rinsing, rub the contents of 1 container plain yogurt into your hair. Leave on for half an hour. Then rinse it all out with cool water. Style or set as usual. For optimum results, let your hair dry naturally, without added heat.

Chapter 6

Here's to Your Hair!

Your hair is your crowning glory—an old description, but a true one. The texture and sheen of hair make it naturally exciting. Today, the art of haircutting and the sophistication of hairstyling tools and products make it possible for every woman to wear the style that truly complements her looks.

Do you have a striking profile? Consider wearing your hair very, very short to show it off.

For a taller look, wear an upswept style to give you a few inches of extra height.

A rigid style that doesn't move no matter what you do makes any woman look older. Aim for that attractive look of careless care—well-groomed, yet relaxed.

Are you petite? Keep to a fairly short length—not below your chin—and a neat shape. Otherwise, you'll be overwhelmed by a mass of hair.

Gray hair must have a contemporary cut. With a fussy style, you'll look very old-ladyish.

Pale blond, carroty red and black hair generally look best when styled simply. Avoid overdone looks, since your hair color provides all the drama you need.

Gray hair looks best in soft waves or straight—but not super-curly. Avoid very frizzy hairdos.

Look years younger by styling a soft, touchable pullback, not a severe, matronly bun.

Tall women in ultra-short hairdos can look like pinheads. Choose a medium-length or long style to balance your height.

If you wear glasses, you've got enough covering your face without long bangs, temple waves or cheek curls. Keep your hairstyle simple and off your face.

Counteract the downward pull of facial lines and wrinkles with a style that sweeps hair up at the temples. Try feathered, brushed-back sides.

Very low hairlines are a problem. Think about having the line raised permanently by electrolysis. If this is not a possibility, you can disguise your hairline with full or sideswept bangs that cover it.

A delicate, heart-shaped face needs balance for its narrow chin. Good styles for you feature curly bangs, fluffed curls behind the ears, sideswept bangs, a side part or a close crown.

Pear-shaped faces are narrow on top, wide at the jaw. You can balance the shape with a style that has width at the temples or wide bangs. Cheek curls and wavy sides that cut the line of your jaw are good, too. So is a short, full cut.

To make a long face seem shorter, think about wearing long bangs or a deep brow dip. Another excellent idea is curly sides—perhaps achieved with a perm if you've got fine locks—that add the illusion of greater width. Your style should never cover your cheeks and temples.

On a square face, you need to soften those angles. Soft side waves, bangs and cheek curls all do this. Height on top and width at the jawline visually change the shape of your face.

Flattering styles for a round face feature sleek sides that don't add any extra width—like a straight, one-length blunt cut. Forehead tendrils or wispy bangs will make your shape less moonlike, and anything asymmetrical—a side part, sideswept bangs, off-center ponytails and chignons—will do the same trick. Good on you is extra height but no added width.

Do you have the classic oval face? Luckily, you can wear most hairstyles, so pick one you love. Go with your hair texture, not against it.

A prominent nose seems less noticeable when the main emphasis is at the back of the head. Fullness at the crown with fluffy layers, a crown chignon or ponytail will give balance. Avoid a middle part, which draws the eye straight down to your nose.

Soft, fluffy bangs will balance a receding chin. Secure your sides back with combs or barrettes so the distance between your small chin and ear will appear greater.

Slim a double chin with height and fullness at your crown. A permed and layered cut would work. So would a natural curly look that's full at the crown. Don't wear your hair longer than medium length—too long will drag the emphasis down where you don't want it at all!

Prominent or jutting chins also need fullness in back for balance. Think about wavy layers or a perm. Avoid bangs or brow dips.

Make a long neck seem less skinny with hair that's long enough to fall gracefully around it in back and at the sides.

Lengthen a very short neck with a hairstyle that is short or swept up—in other words, off your nape. Show as much of your neck as possible. Low necklines, by the way, will also enhance this effect.

Medium brown, light brown and sandy-colored hair generally look best in a more complicated style, for example, waves or curly layers. Since your hair color isn't dramatic, your style can be. Avoid a too-tailored cut or severe, geometric lines.

Long layers give curly hair more flexibility. You can wear it curly, or you can easily blow it dry for a smoother look.

A blunt cut adds bounce to thin or fine hair. A blunt cut has hair cut all one length or in sections that are one length, like a Dutch-boy bob with bangs.

If your hair grows forward from the crown, consider wearing long bangs so your locks can do their thing— which is to fall forward.

A good shape for stubborn, wiry hair is close to the head where its crispness holds a perfect line.

Naturally frizzy-curly hair will behave better if the top and sides are kept fairly short.

Have a perm if you've got thin hair and live in a humid climate. A perm will thicken your hair, and your style won't go flat with the dampness.

You *can* trim one-length hair by yourself, if you're

careful. For a style that's longer at the sides and shorter in back, gather your hair in a low ponytail at the nape of the neck. Using a sharp haircutting scissors, cut the ponytail straight across to the length desired.

Plait lots of skinny braids into your just-washed hair. Tie ribbons on the ends. When this kicky set dries, you'll have a headful of silky waves.

Create original hair ornaments by gluing old "jewels," beads and Cracker Jack prizes to plain five-and-dime barrettes.

Weave enameled chopsticks through a neatly coiled topknot. Use two sticks and make an X through the knot. Can't get your hands on these accessories? Paint chopsticks from your local Chinese restaurant with bright enamel. Or use pickup sticks.

Roll a smooth pompadour over a short cotton sock. Trim the sock to the length you want. Twist it and pin the ends in place. Brush sections of hair over the sock, one at a time, and pin in place. Spray for a neat, unbroken line.

Do you crave a long-hair look but love your easy shortie? Slick all your hair back from the brow and sides and wrap a thick, fake braid around your head, like a headband.

Wear four or six barrettes at a time. Clip strands back with matching pairs, or place barrettes randomly all over your head.

Be a seductive Scarlett O'Hara with a fragrant flower pinned over your ear. Perfect is one gardenia, but daisies are disarming, too!

Tie a flower to your braid. Attach a rose or a tiger lily to the end of your braid with a "Baggie" tie. The flower can be fresh from the garden or never-wilt silk.

Asymmetry is interesting. Wear an off-center chignon high on your crown. Or you can gather your ponytail over one shoulder and leave the other bare. For shorter hair, get that off-center fashion look by clipping one side of your style back off your face with a beautiful comb.

Instead of combs or barrettes, secure your long hair away from your face by lifting out two side sections at your temples and twisting them into two long rope-coils. Now bring these back and pin them together at the back of your head.

Soften a too-severe style with tendrils of curls. Use a cuticle scissors to snip two-inch strands around the face. Set these delicate wisps in big clip curls, then brush out gently.

A glamour movie look: Gather your hair in a ponytail and roll the ends on hot rollers. You'll get a style that's polished at the crown and curled at the ends.

How about one big barrette, clipped vertically in back, to hold a long, lush ponytail?

Be creative with your combs. Secure a beautiful one above your chignon. Use double combs to sweep hair back off to one side. Pull back your bangs with one curvy comb. Be imaginative.

Considering a radical hair color change? Buy a wig in the shade you're thinking about, and wear it every day, everywhere for two entire weeks. See if you really love the color for keeps. The price of the wig might just save you money and heartache in the long run— or save you needless anxiety.

Experts suggest changing your hair color to within three shades of your own color. You'll get the most believable results.

Set a kitchen timer or an alarm clock when coloring your hair. Minutes make a difference, so don't get distracted.

Brighten dark brown hair with red or light brown highlights, but not with blond, which is too harsh and fake-looking.

By highlighting more at the sides than on top, you can widen a long face. The added lightness gives the illusion of more width.

If your face is round, highlight only the brow area and not the sides. The brightness on top will give the illusion of more height.

Gray hair looks good if you happen to have a fair or a very dark complexion. If your skin is beige or sallow, consider blonding your gray head with hair color. If you have only a bit of gray, highlighting it can create a striking effect.

Mix neutral henna to a creamy consistency with strong, freshly brewed coffee that's been cooled, and you'll add beautiful, burnished highlights to dark hair.

Add burgundy highlights to dark brown by applying neutral henna mixed with grape juice. Test on a few strands first to seee if you like the tint.

Give your blond or light brown hair a glorious burst of sunlight: highlight only very fine pieces of hair on your top layers.

With olive skin, avoid a pale blond hair color.

Ruddy complexions look prettiest in "cool" shades like ash blond or ash brown. Avoid the warm, reddish tones. They'll only make your skin appear more florid.

Pale ivory skin seems more lively with a golden or strawberry blond color. Avoid the cool "ash" shades which will wash out your skin.

To color and perm at same time overtaxes the hair. Perm first, then wait one week to do hair coloring.

Give your new hair color two or three days before deciding you don't like it. Let your hair's natural oils "settle" the color.

With new hair color, you may need new makeup colors. Shop for the shades that complement your hair —foundation, lipstick and blusher—and consider it part of your overall investment.

Color your hair *before* a vacation in the sun. If you do it after you return, you'll get uneven results. The top layers will be more porous from exposure to the sun, and they'll take more color than the underlayers.

Herbal hair lightener: Boil 2 cups of water. Steep 5 camomile tea bags. Add the juice of 2 lemons and let cool. Rinse the brew through your tresses before sunbathing.

Chemically lightened hair should be protected from

the sun with a floppy beach hat. The sun will alter your color via oxidation.

Don't panic! You can correct a too-brassy hair color with a temporary drabbing rinse in a cool ash shade.

If your hair lightening experiment went too far and you're much too light, correct the color with a temporary rinse in a darker, more flattering shade.

Camouflage disastrous color (or cut) with a wig. You can look fashionably pretty as you let your new hair grow in. Take this time to restore your hair to good condition.

Indulge yourself and take your wig to the hairdresser for a styling. Put it on and have your stylist design a look that's more natural than the way it came out of the box and just right for your face.

Deepen an old blond wig's color with a temporary hair rinse. Follow the coloring directions on the box.

For a super-smooth look, wear an old nylon stocking under your wig.

Want your wig to look authentic? Sleep in it for a tousled effect.

Shampoo your wig according to the directions that came with it. Rinse well, shake the wig out and hang it to dry away from the heat.

Hats create instant glamour. With long hair, sport a French beret. With a short cut, wear a cuffed knit cap. With a wide, curly style, try a hood. And with a ponytail, how about a man's bowler?

Don't leave a special occasion hairstyle to chance. Rehearse it just as you try on your outfit. And like your dress, alter it if you need to. Get a trim or a fresh hair accessory. Remember, a perfect hair look makes a perfect fashion look.

Cut out magazine pictures and bring them to your hairdresser. From a photo, your stylist can get a good idea of what you want.

Local hairdressing schools and salons sometimes offer free haircuts, shampoos and sets. Be prepared to have a student do the work—under supervision, of course.

Get haircuts more frequently in summer. Hair grows faster in warmer weather than in cold.

If your hair gets greasy very quickly, check your diet. It may be possible to control the situation at least somewhat by cutting down on fats and oils.

Rinse hair thoroughly as soon as you step out of a swimming pool. Chlorine damages and discolors the hair. If your hair is permed or colored, be sure to wear a bathing cap.

Use coated plastic bands, and never rubber bands, on your hair. Rubber bands stretch and break strands.

Combat electricity by rubbing your hairbrush with a sheet of fabric softener. It works on your comb, too.

Don't pour shampoo over your hair from the bottle. Measure it as the bottle suggests—just a capful is usually enough for a washing. Keep in mind that saturating your hair with shampoo can strip out too much natural oil. Plus, it's hard to rinse all that shampoo out if you've used too much.

Rainwater—pure and natural—is the best shampoo water ever. Keep a large, clean bucket outdoors to catch it. After a downpour, bottle your treasure and use it for shampooing and rinsing.

Egg is a wonderful protein shampoo. Beat the whites of 2 eggs to stiffness. Fold in the 2 yolks. Wet your hair and massage the "shampoo" in. Rinse well. You might divide the mixture in half and wash twice.

When shampooing, massage your scalp with the pads of your fingertips. Don't scratch with your nails. Wet hair is delicate, so treat it gently.

Shampoo booster for dark hair: Add 1 beaten egg yolk to your regular shampoo and wash as usual.

Shampoo booster for light hair: Add 1 beaten egg white to your regular shampoo. Wash as usual.

New Year's Day shampoo: Start your year in high style with a refreshing shower and shampoo. Rinse your strands with leftover champagne. It will add loads of body and make you feel like keeping those resolutions!

A corn-row hairstyle can take hours to create. Nevertheless, you must undo it to shampoo thoroughly every week. Between washings, quick-clean your scalp with a cotton ball moistened in witch hazel.

In the shower and out of shampoo? In a pinch, you can use your bath soap, but be sure to rinse very well and follow up with a conditioning treatment.

For oily hair and dandruff: Alternate a dandruff shampoo with a formula for oily hair. Shampoo every other day.

Do-it-yourself dandruff shampoo: Crush a dozen aspirins and blend into your shampoo bottle. Shampoo as usual, massaging your scalp thoroughly and leaving the shampoo on your hair for 5 minutes. Rinse very well with cool water.

If you're frazzled and can't shampoo, just wash your bangs in the sink. You'll feel a lot fresher.

Instant shampoo idea: Sprinkle some baking soda on a hairbrush. Brush through your hair.

If you're in a rush and can't wash your hair when it really needs it, sprinkle cornstarch lightly through your hair, then brush. The powdery starch works as "instant shampoo," blotting up oils and restoring some amount of bounce.

A fragrant hair rinse for brunettes is cinnamon tea. Steep 3 cinnamon sticks in 2 cups of boiled water for 20 minutes. Strain and cool. Use after shampooing.

For added shine, follow up your shampoo with an apple cider vinegar rinse. Mix 4 tablespoons of vinegar in a cup of water, and pour over your hair as a final rinse.

For special party nights, add a few sprays of sweet cologne to your final shampoo rinse. Or refresh your set by misting hair with a cologne atomizer, then roller-setting or refreshing with a hot comb.

After shampooing, you should protect your hair by first blotting up excess water with a dry towel, *then* blowing it dry. The idea is to minimize your blow-drying time since, handy as the blow-dryer is, it does contribute to hair dryness.

Between shampoos, wipe excess oil from your scalp with an astringent-moistened cotton puff.

Treat your hair and scalp to a deep conditioning. Warm your hair conditioner in a double boiler, then use your fingertips to work it gently into your scalp and strands. Wrap your head, helmet-style, with a length of aluminum foil or plastic wrap to keep in the heat. After one hour, remove the cap and rinse. Allow your hair and scalp to air-dry.

Brighten a dull-looking perm by slicking hairdressing cream over those frizzy curls. Give it a light dressing, so hair will look shiny but not greasy.

Extra-rich conditioner: Beat ¼–½ cup olive oil (depending on your hair's length) together with 2 whole eggs. Apply to your hair. After an hour, rinse out and shampoo hair in warm water.

Coax frizzy, dried-out hair back to health by conditioning for fifteen minutes before every shampoo. Watch for signs of improvement.

Prevent split ends by rubbing conditioner into your hair's ends. Leave it on as long as you can before shampooing.

After shampooing, hair is very delicate. Comb with a wide-toothed comb, which is far less likely to tear or break your strands than a fine-toothed one.

Give a lift to limp hair by setting with flat beer. You can also use a mixture of 1 teaspoon gelatin mixed with 1 cup boiling water, after it has cooled.

Emergency setting lotion: Comb the white of an egg through your wet hair. Set and be sure to brush your dry style well.

If you ordinarily roller-set and are stuck without rollers, substitute round cotton balls. Wrap hair around the cotton, and secure with toothpicks.

Blow-dry hair with a "warm" or "cool" temperature. These are safest. "Hot" is too drying for most hair and can lead to dryness.

As you blow-dry, run your fingers through your hair for a full, fluffy look.

For fine hair, blow-dry from underneath. Bend over from the waist and dry the bottom layers first. When hair is almost dry, stand up and go over the top layers. Rule of thumb: You'll always get more fullness blow-drying in the opposite direction to your comb-out.

Use end papers with electric rollers to avoid knots

and tangles. You can make your own with half sheets of toilet tissue.

Make those curls last! Set with hot rollers, then shower and the steam will make your curls take. Wear a shower cap, of course.

Hot rollers can't be used on wet hair. Let your hair dry first (or use a blow-dryer).

On hair that's been chemically treated (colored or permed), cut down on your hot-roller setting time. Treated hair is more porous and takes the set quicker than virgin hair.

To avoid "fishhooks" when using a curling rod, make sure you clamp the rod on the very ends of your strands. No hair should be sticking out at all.

Revive droopy bangs with a curling iron when the weather is rainy or the humidity is high. You can curl a ponytail with a rod, too. If you're going out directly after work, you might tuck the rod into your shoulder bag for touching up your hairdo. Most of these appliances are slim and small enough to fit easily.

When curling short hair near the face with a curling rod, slip a comb under the rod to protect your bare skin.

If you use a blow-dryer, hot rollers or a curling rod, you must deep-condition weekly and use a conditioning rinse after every shampoo. These hair tools are terrific, but they can leave your hair parched without replenishing treatments.

Tame loose strands escaping from that oh-so-neat coif by misting hairspray on a cotton puff and rubbing lightly over the flyaways.

Don't buy a synthetic-bristle brush with sharp tips. If they feel sharp to your fingers, think what they'll do to your hair (tear the strands or scratch your scalp).

Soft-bristle brushes are gentle on fine hair. Use a stiffer bristle for thicker hair.

Give dry hair lots of brushing. Those long strokes from scalp to ends distribute the scalp's oils along the hair shafts and help a dry condition. If you want to, use two hair brushes, alternating them rhythmically— one in each hand.

Clean your brushes whenever you shampoo. Swish them around in mild soap suds, then rinse with warm water and dry over a towel, bristles down. Keep away from direct heat. Or you can soak your brushes and combs in ¼ cup baking soda in a basin of hot water. After 5 minutes, rinse and set to dry.

One clever way to remove dirt from a comb is with buttonhole thread. Slide the thread between the teeth —like dental floss.

Chapter 7

The Fun of Fragrance

Perfume has the ability to bring romance into a woman's life every day of the week. A dab of a favorite scent behind the ears, at the throat or on the wrists can lift the spirits instantaneously and make even mundane tasks like dishwashing and mending more pleasant. A truly magnificent fragrance can transform the moment and etch it indelibly in memory. If you haven't yet experienced the joy of fragrance, you're in for a treat. Dip in, starting with these hints.

Before you decide to buy, test any perfume or cologne on your skin. Rub a drop on the inside of your wrist, then wait an hour for your body heat to make the scent "bloom." If you still like it, plunk down your money.

When to refresh your cologne? About every four hours.

Light flower and fruit scents are perfect for summertime. Pick lemon, lime, pine lavender, white rose or lilac. Avoid the heady, musky perfumes that overpower when it's hot.

A marvelous man's cologne is sometimes great on

a woman, especially if you want a scent none of your friends are wearing. Just because it's in a "man's" bottle doesn't mean you can't love it as much as he does!

Don't spray perfume over your jewelry. The perfume oils will discolor gold, pearls and other gems. Fragrance first, then jewelry.

In summer, cologne stored in the refrigerator will feel cool and tingly when you splash it on after your shower or bath.

Wear a gardenia in your hair. At night and for parties, it's a purely romantic look—and a natural perfume.

Spray cologne lightly on the inside hem of your dress or skirt and let the scent rise about you. Don't spray outside, since cologne may discolor some fabrics.

Tuck a perfumed handkerchief into your purse. Dab a spot of perfume oil on a pretty lacy square— just be sure the oil matches or complements your own cologne.

Swimming in salt or chlorinated water washes cologne away. Apply after a swim, not before.

Layer fragrance with soap, body powder and

cologne all in the same scent. All the different forms of it will give your fragrance a richer impact, perfect for that special evening.

Don't keep your colognes on a sunny dresser top. Fragrances will turn when exposed to too much heat.

During menstruation, many women experience a change in their sense of smell. Be aware of this, and don't overapply perfume at this time of the month.

Instant sachet: a cake of gorgeously perfumed soap. Unwrap it, and let the soap nestle among your favorite things in a dresser drawer.

Don't spend extra money on a small perfume for your shoulder bag. Buy an atomizer at the dime store and decant your regular fragrance into it.

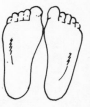

Want an instant lift? Spray the soles of your feet with cologne.

Even empty perfume bottles continue to dispense their mysterious fragrance. Place that just-finished bottle in your lingerie drawer to sweeten your prettiest underthings.

Get extra mileage from a near-empty perfume or cologne flask by adding one or two drops of alcohol to the bottle. Or pour in a little vodka!

Sew tiny clove sachets for your lingerie drawer. Use a flowered print or gingham checks. Cut two 3″ squares. Place right sides together and stitch along three sides, ¼″ from edge. Turn right sides out. Fill with cloves. Turn edges of fourth side in and stitch closed.

Instant potpourri? Toss a handful of cloves, allspice and whole nutmeg into a scarf square, knot it and tuck between your sweaters.

Add a few drops of cologne to the final rinse water when you wash delicate underthings.

Perfumed oils are intense. Dab them on sparingly since a little bit goes a long, long way.

Create your own "private label" cologne. Dilute your favorite perfume oil—like lemon, jasmine, sandalwood or rose—with rubbing alcohol. Add as much alcohol as you wish for a stronger or lighter cologne.

For active sports, wear perfumed body powder. You'll get more staying power than with cologne, which tends to slide off the skin as you perspire.

Create a zesty orange bath oil. Shake in a bottle: 3 ounces of orange extract and 3 ounces of safflower oil. Refrigerate and each time you bathe, add a capful to your tub.

Make a sachet necklace for Valentine's Day: Cut two matching hearts from a pretty red-and-white flowered gingham. Make them just a bit bigger than you want the "locket" to be. Sew them together, leaving a ½" opening. Turn the seams inside. Now, through the opening, insert cloves, bits of cinnamon stick, dried flowers—any combinaton of aromatic ingredients you like. Sew up the opening, and stitch a narrow red satin ribbon "necklace" to the heart.

Splash cologne on your body *after* your bath or shower. When your skin is slightly damp and warm, the fragrance will cling better.

Apply perfume sparingly in the morning. Early in the day, you are less sensitive to smells than in the afternoon and evening. It's easy to overdo your fragrance because you're less aware of the effect. (Ever sit next to a heavily perfumed woman on the bus to work?)

Don't test more than three fragrances at one time. Beyond that, you get "olfactory overload"—in other words, you won't be able to distinguish any other scents at all.

Oily skin tends to alter fragrance more than dry skin. If you're oily, steer clear of the ultra-delicate scents, like light florals. They'll change too much on you. Go for the richer, headier colognes and perfumes.

Don't buy perfume because you liked it on a friend. Fragrance smells very different on people because of different body chemistries. You really must test the scent on your own skin.

Chapter 8

Beauty Potpourri

Here, a grab bag of helpful hints. Tips galore, there's something here for everybody.

Get to know your looks by examining your face and body in the mirror from every angle. Study the good features and the bad. When you really know yourself, you'll have an easier time picking makeup and fashions that work.

Makeup brushes can be stored prettily in a 6-ounce frozen-juice tin you've painted or covered with adhesive-backed paper.

When temperatures soar, keep your makeup cool. When it's above 85° F., store cosmetics in a cool, dry spot (how about your fridge?) for refreshing, easy application.

Keep skin, hair, teeth, nails and body meticulously clean and fresh at all times. Good grooming doesn't cost money, yet it's the most important beauty secret of all.

In the morning, do your face, then hop into a lukewarm tub. The moist heat from the bath will set your makeup to look fresh and natural.

Have your picture snapped in each new hairdo and makeup look you try out. Photos are great for evaluating new looks and deciding which ones worked— and which didn't.

When you are having a portrait done by a photographer, face the camera at a three-quarter angle, more flattering than a straight-on shot. Show your better side, tilt your chin up a bit, relax those shoulders . . . and smile.

Key your makeup style to your personality. Vivacious types will love bold, "look-at-me" makeup, but if you're rather shy, you'll feel happier in a softer, quieter look.

When someone makes fun of you for trying to improve your looks, ignore him or her. Beauty is an ancient and glorious art that lets every woman—no matter how rich or poor—visually express her many moods and faces.

Keep cosmetics, makeup brushes and miscellaneous supplies together. Organization will make your mornings calmer with less frenetic rushing around.

Break out of boring beauty ruts. Do you always wear blue eyeshadow? Do you always part your hair in

the middle? Some habits are due to sheer laziness!
Try some fashionable ideas you think might be fun.

Feel daring? Accent your décolletage by subtly
brushing powder blusher into your cleavage.

Night lighting is generally softer and dimmer than
daylight. Wear more intense makeup in stronger colors. Wear more of it, too.

Practice new beauty habits faithfully. For instance,
if you start to moisturize your skin or condition your
hair or exercise, it might take several weeks before you
notice results. Keep up the effort in the meantime.

Hard-water hint: Use a nonsoap cleanser and a
soapless shampoo. After washing, rinse skin and hair
very well so no residue remains. A worthwhile beauty
investment would be a water purifier that attaches to
your bathroom faucet.

Trial sizes of some skin-care products and cosmetics are available in many discount drug centers. If it's
possible, test any product you're thinking of buying in
this money-saving size. See how you like it, then invest
in the big size.

Create your own beauty work space with a plastic
cutting board that fits over your bathroom sink.
Spread out your makeup and have fun.

Buy makeup, skin-care and hair-care products that work for *you*—not for your sister, mother or friend. It will take a bit of time before you discover them all, but if you pursue the search, you'll end up with a tailor-made beauty kit, like the one you'd get from a beauty professional.

Check your profiles—left and right—after making up and doing your hair. Fix anything that doesn't look wonderful from the side, too.

Make up in natural light. Set your mirror near a window, if possible. Next best light is regular light bulbs, but not fluorescent. They are too harsh and distort color too much.

Don't hesitate to return any cosmetic or skin-care product if there is a real problem. An allergic reaction, a package that falls apart, a product that dries out . . . take it back. If the store won't exchange it or refund your money, write directly to the manufacturer.

Organize your makeup in a plastic kitchen-utensil drawer organizer.

If you are color-blind and have trouble distinguishing makeup shades, mark all your cosmetics not already labeled with a tiny adhesive label that tells you exactly what the color is.

Highlight a barebacked dress with a "jewel" pasted at your shoulder. Take a colorful stone from an old necklace or bracelet, and affix it with surgical adhesive.

Keep fluffy cotton balls in a glass candy jar on your bathroom shelf.

Before an important occasion, mastermind your own makeover—a complete redo. Get a new hairdo, new makeup, a brand-new image. Get your new look together at least two weeks before the event so you won't feel strange when you make your grand entrance!

The advantage to a "beauty club" is that you can test lots of different makeup and perfume. To offset the cost, split one membership with a friend—and share the products.

Alcohol cleans cosmetic brushes. Dip them in rubbing alcohol, swish around, then gently dry with a tissue. Brushes should get the once-over every other week.

Pick up a glamorous forties or fifties compact in a thrift store. If you can, replace the powder, and you'll have a one-of-a-kind powder dispenser for your purse. If you can't find the right-size powder, just use the mirror for lipstick touch-ups.

Rule of thumb: Spend as much time removing your makeup as you do putting it on.

Makeup is really quite versatile. You can use lipstick as eyeshadow (if you like the color), cheek color as lipstick and bronzer as lip gloss. Read the package. Unless it warns against using on certain areas (eyes, for instance), feel free to exercise your creativity.

Don't forget the dime stores when you're buying makeup. Frequently they sell their own cosmetic brands at incredibly low prices.

Have you always wished for freckles? Apply farm-girl freckles over your foundation with light brown eyebrow pencil. Dot them randomly on your nose and cheeks. Then press each spot with your index finger so it blends with your base. Last, dust with loose powder.

Don't moisten eyeliner or any cosmetic with saliva. Use water—it's more sanitary and doesn't promote the growth of bacteria.

Key your appearance to your age. Not that a forty-year-old need look sedate, but she ought to avoid trying to look like her teenage daughter. Neither should a high school student try to pass for a career woman. Look your age—every year has its special charm.

Add razzle-dazzle to backless shoes. Apply a beautiful decal at the back of your ankle when you go out dancing or partying. Decals are temporary beautifiers you can buy at cosmetic counters or through some mail order companies.

Sprinkle your lacy undies with scented dusting powder before stepping into them.

What shape's your face? Pull all your hair back and stand before a mirror. Using an old eyebrow pencil, follow the contours of your face in the mirror. Study the outline to see if it's mostly oval, round, oblong, square, heart or pear.

Discourage frown lines. Paste strips of hairset tape between your eyebrows, and every time you furrow your brows, you'll feel a reminding tug.

Copy the pro makeup artists and use a fishing tackle box for storing your cosmetics.

Must for every woman's handbag: lipstick, blusher, powder, a perfume atomizer and a comb.

Remove every last bit of jewelry cleaner from your rings, necklaces and bracelets. Cleaner not completely washed off may cause skin irritations.

Buy calamine, aspirin and antiseptic creams in

small sizes. After a year, these become outdated and
need to be replaced.

Fluorescent lighting drains the color from your
skin. In the office, check your makeup under the
light. Correct it, if you need to. Usually, what you'll
need is more blusher.

Have a date a half hour after work? Remove your
face makeup—foundation, blusher, lipstick and powder—and reapply it. But leave your eye makeup alone.
Just touch up your shadow by adding a bit more
color.

Make more space on your vanity top by storing
all your makeup on a lazy Susan—the two-tiered kind
that will give you twice as much room!

Chick makeup box: Cover a sturdy shoebox with
gold or silver self-stick paper, inside and out.

Buy a kitchen timer. Use it for doing your hair-
color, clocking facial masks or timing your exercise
workouts. Buy a pretty one just for beauty routines.
Borrowing your kitchen timer might result in a superb
shade of blond, but a burnt Sunday roast!

How much to tip your hairdresser or manicurist?

The practice varies from city to city, from salon to salon. If you don't know, feel free to ask the receptionist if tipping is customary, and if it is, what a usual tip is. When in doubt, tip 10–15 percent of your total bill.

Chapter 9
Bath and Body

Of course, we bathe to get clean. But a bath or shower can also invigorate or relax the body and mind, depending on how we approach it. Adding just a few drops of aromatic oil or some choice herbs, for instance, can make bathing a special part of your day to treasure. In this chapter, you'll also find hints for the body—ideas for head-to-toe pampering that will leave your body as smooth as silk.

Once a week, enjoy a pampering "spa night" in your tub. Do all those nice extra things, like pumicing rough spots, conditioning your hair, masking your complexion and pushing cuticles back with a facecloth.

Bath is a terrific time for hairsetting. Roll or pincurl dry hair, then relax in a warm tub. The steam will set your style. This trick works in the shower, too. Wear a loose-fitting shower cap that lets some steam in.

Your ideal bath temperature is between 96° and 98° F.—body temperature. A warm bath is the most relaxing and healthful temperature.

Hot baths are stimulating, but keep them short

(between five and ten minutes) as excess heat can be debilitating. If you have a heart condition, or you are pregnant or your doctor advises against them, avoid hot tubs altogether.

Quick sponge: Saturate a bath sponge with bay rum and rub over your body, from head to toe.

Use a bath brush. If you are plagued by blackheads or pimples on your back, lather with a medicated soap. Rinse well with water and splash on astringent.

Alleviate muscular aches with a warm soak for fifteen minutes. Follow up with a camphorated oil rubdown over the sore spots.

Add a cup of dry powdered milk to your tub to reduce itchiness.

Stitch up "bran bags" to soften hard water. Cut cheesecloth into 5" squares. Stitch two squares together on three sides. Fill the bag with clean bran and sew the fourth side. Toss one bag into your bathwater each time you bathe.

Luxuriate in a strawberry soak. Blend 1 pound of fresh strawberries and 1 ounce of white vinegar. Let the mixture stand 10 days. Strain through cheesecloth into a jar. Cover and refrigerate. Dribble a bit into your running bathwater.

Cleanse naturally with baking soda. Add one cupful to your tub and soak dirt away—no soap necessary at all.

Take a health spa vacation in your tub. Pour half a cup of sea salt into your bath and soak for ten minutes. Your skin will be rosy and glowing when you step out. Since salt may be irritating to some sensitive skins, test this one out by sitting on the edge of the tub and first soaking just your calves. If you have no adverse reaction, hop in.

For super-soft skin, pamper your body with a milk bath. To a tub half-filled with warm water, add 1 cup powdered milk and ¼ cup of baby oil.

Slice a fresh orange into your bathwater for a refreshing summer afternoon bath. Or you may prefer to nibble on the flesh of the orange as you splash in bathwater perfumed with only the rind!

Dry skin regimen: Soak in a warm tub for fifteen minutes, using a super-fatted soap for washing. Pat your body dry with a towel and immediately rub lanolin over the dry areas. Dust with powder to make the lanolin less sticky. Repeat every night until you notice improvement. (Note: You can buy lanolin at the drugstore.)

Set a snack table by your tub to hold all your supplies. In a big bathroom, you can keep it standing permanently. If your room is tiny, fold the table against the wall when not in use.

If your skin is scaly, bathe or shower only every other day. On alternate days, enjoy a sponge bath.

Don't rub your wet body vigorously. Pat it dry gently, since wet skin is delicate.

Firm your thighs in the tub. First raise your right leg, grasp the calf and pull the leg in toward your body. Release it, and repeat the exercise with your left leg.

Bathtub waist-stretcher: Sit facing the long side of the tub with your legs crossed. Hold the edge of the tub with your left hand. Raise your right arm overhead and bounce sideways to the left. Repeat to the other side.

Lower-back-stretcher: Sit with your legs and arms stretched out straight in front of you. "Pulse" forward from hips, reaching for the opposite wall with your fingertips.

Make a comfy bath pillow with a child's plastic swim tube. Tie a 2' length of drapery sash cord (in a color to match your bathroom) around the tube, knotting the ends together. Hang the tube by this cord on a large self-stick hook, and position the hook on the wall above the head of your tub. Let the pillow fall at a good height to cushion your head as you lie back in the tub. When you've found the comfortable position, attach the hook permanently to the wall.

An instant bath pillow: Fold a large bath towel in half lengthwise, then roll it up and prop behind your neck as you luxuriate in the tub.

Stitch a terry bath mitt, using your hand as a pattern. Cut the glove 1½" larger than your hand. Sew the two pieces together with a ½" seam. Fill the glove with soap chips from used bars. In the shower, just wet the mitt and suds up.

Use that last drop of shampoo. Float the near-empty plastic bottle in your bathtub. You'll enjoy a thrifty bubble bath.

Make a "bath vanity" to hold your beauty goodies while you bathe. Cut a piece of shelving board a bit longer than your tub's width. Sand it and paint with polyurethane or cover with waterproof shelf paper. When you bathe, lay the board across your tub and set out your mirror, tweezers, face mask, hair pack, pumice. . . .

Stitch up an after-bath cover-up—it's easy. Select a pretty bath sheet and seam the two short sides together. With the seam inside, turn the top edge in 1½" and hem it, making a casing. Leave 1" unstitched on the casing. Slip 1" elastic through, gather to a

comfortable underarm length and sew the elastic ends together. Finish the casing hem.

How about an unwinding bath? Put the workday behind you by stripping off your clothes as soon as you get home. Step into a richly bubbled and perfumed tub that clears your mind of everything and gives your body a chance to really r-e-l-a-x. . . .

Follow your soap-and-water shower with a Japanese-style soak in a bathtub filled with clean warm water. Add scented oil and relax for ten minutes. Lightly towel dry, then lubricate your body. This is wonderful for dry skin, since the extra soak plumps your skin with moisture which you then seal in with your body lotion.

Enjoy a sparkling tub. Add a large bottle of club soda to your bath for that bubbly, get-up-and-go feeling.

Give yourself a breast exam in the bath or shower. Hold your fingers flat together, and make gentle circular motions in a clockwise direction. Circle over every part of both breasts. Note any bumps that are not normal for you. After you've dried yourself off, look at your breasts in the mirror. Check for changes in shape or size. Note any dimpling of the skin or change in your nipples. Check with your arms down, then lifted. This examination should be done the week after your period ends. Report any changes to your doctor. Most changes are normal, but you'll feel better knowing that for sure.

Make your antiperspirant last longer by first swabbing underams with cotton pads soaked in witch
hazel. Towel dry, then apply deodorant.

Baking soda is an effective and mild deodorant.
Dust it under your arms as needed.

Bleach very dark body hair on the arms, legs and
tummy in two separate sessions, rather than keep a
potentially irritating bleach on your skin for too long.
Bleach once, then wait twenty-four hours to do it
again.

Never shave your arms—the regrowth is prickly.
Instead, bleach dark hair so it's less obvious.

Before going for electrolysis, make sure your super-
fluous hair isn't due to pregnancy, the Pill or a medication. In these cases, hair growth may be temporary.
Consult your doctor.

Dark tummy hair can spoil your bare bikini line.
Don't tweeze, but bleach these strands carefully with
a facial-strength hair lightener.

When depilating around the bikini leg line, wear
a pair of old panties to make sure you take off just
the hair that needs taking off.

Ten minutes before shaving your legs, presoften the skin with body lotion. You'll get the silkiest shave ever and your legs will feel wonderful.

Go extra slowly over ankles, knees and shins when shaving. These bony areas are easily nicked if you rush the job.

To help break up lumpy "cellulite" by improving circulation, gently stroke the bumpy, fatty areas once a day with your open palms. Use baby oil, and always stroke toward the heart.

Use body lotion to massage your legs. Start at the toes. Work to the instep, then massage ankles, calves, knees and finally the thighs. Massage every day to zip up the blood flow and banish that heavy-legged feeling.

Create a wonderful massage oil by mixing equal parts avocado, mineral and olive oils.

Do massage your breasts lightly. Increasing the blood flow gives them a toned and healthy appearance. Use an oil, and rub gently with your fingertips.

If you find baby oil or vegetable oils too thick to use on your body, thin them with water. Mix half and half, and shake well before applying.

For easy application, pour baby oil into a plastic plant-misting bottle. You'll waste less when spraying it over your body.

Slough old skin cells from your body with a mixture of avocado oil and salt. Rub into the skin gently on a washcloth. Rinse off and wash with soap and water.

Make up your own sweet body oil. Fill a pottery jar with safflower oil. Add a few vanilla beans. After one day, strain. For a stronger oil, add fresh beans and repeat the procedure.

Soften calloused elbows by resting them in two grapefruit halves. Squeeze out the juice first (and sip it for extra vitamin C), then sit with your elbows in the shells for 15–20 minutes.

Chapter 10

Beautiful Hands and Feet

A graceful hand is the sign of a gracious woman, and a perfectly groomed foot reflects the pride she takes in her body. Even if your hands are subject to the roughest treatment in the world—as women's hands frequently are—you can follow some of these easy steps to keep them soft and holdable. And there's nothing like a monthly pedicure for boosting your morale and making you feel totally pampered.

File your nails *before* washing or bathing, when they are hard and firm. After a bath, they're too soft and subject to tearing.

Once a week, buff polish-free nails to shine them and encourage growth. First, soak in a shallow dish filled with warmed olive oil. After five minutes, use a soft chamois cloth or special nail buffer to bring up the natural patina.

Treat dry, peeling fingernails with vitamin E. Prick open a capsule, and rub the oil all over your nails (including the base) to restore lost moisture.

Push cuticles back after your bath—that's when they're softest. Use a soft terry towel and push gently. Don't forget your toenail cuticles.

127

What you eat shows in your nails. Improve their strength and appearance by adding wheat germ and brewer's yeast to your diet. Sprinkle two tablespoons of wheat germ over breakfast cereal or into yogurt, and mix one tablespoon of brewer's yeast in a glass of fruit juice. These supplements, rich in the B vitamins, are sold in health food stores.

Use clippers to trim your nails. Scissors sometimes split and break the nails.

Stop biting your nails! Swab them with the liquid moms buy to discourage kids from sucking their thumbs. When you start to chew, you'll get that bitter taste.

Quick patch for a torn nail: Cover the tear with a tiny piece of tissue paper, and "fasten" the paper in place with a coat of nail polish. Keep the break polished until the nail grows in.

Add one or two drops of red nail polish to a bottle of clear for the faintest blush of a nail color, both pale and delicate.

Make manicures last longer by applying four polish coats in all. First, a base coat, then two color coats and, last, a clear top coat to protect the color.

Unpolished, perfectly groomed nails are elegant.

If your job makes using color impractical, take special care to keep your nails perfectly shaped and buffed to a sheen. Use white pencil under the nail for a meticulous look.

Buff your nails from the cuticle out to the tip. Always go in one direction. Buffing back and forth builds up too much heat, which can damage the nail.

Even when nails are polished, moisturize the nail base and cuticle every night to foster healthy new growth. Massage with petroleum jelly.

If you wear polish constantly, you can avoid yellowish-looking nails by wearing a clear, protective base coat—especially under dark shades. They discolor more than light ones.

Instead of doing a fresh manicure whenever your nail polish chips, just touch up the chips with color.

Speed your polish drying by holding nails under your blow-dryer set on "cool."

Ridges, splits and peeling may be clues to some internal problem or many reflect an allergy to some food or cosmetic. If you notice these, consult your doctor.

Bony hands will look less skinny when nails are

rather short. File them round, not oval, and wear bright polish shades.

Square hands will take on a softer appearance if you grow your nails longer and file them to a pretty, round shape. Avoid vivid colors, but choose subtly interesting tints.

Apply henna to your fingernails for a natural pink polish that won't chip off. Prepare the henna as you would for your hair, and apply it carefully over the nails with a cotton swab or child's small paintbrush. Don't get any on your skin—it stains, remember. The color should last a few weeks, gradually wearing off.

Nail-biters really *can* cultivate gorgeous nails by applying "fakes" and letting their own nails grow out underneath. When nails are as long as you want, remove the top nails and manicure your own perfect set of ten.

Give nails a duo-tone look. Use two complementary colors, a deep red or burgundy and pink or beige. Visualize a diagonal line cutting your nail in two from the base to the end. Polish half the diagonal in the darker color and the other half in the lighter shade.

Good sense for acrylic-nail-wearers: To protect the health of your own nail, make sure the acrylic compound starts at least one-sixteenth of an inch above the nail base.

Apply acrylic nails before you do a complete manicure. Wait until after you apply the solution to push
your cuticles back.

Don't extend your acrylic nails too far beyond the
length you're used to wearing. If you suddenly go
ultra-long, you may find yourself accidentally breaking your new nails.

Have one broken nail ruining your perfect ten?
Extend the offender with a plastic nail tip that's
tacked on with quick-bonding glue. Let your own nail
grow in under it.

Avoid immersing false nails in hot water. Wash
quickly in tepid water and dry well. When doing
dishes, wear rubber gloves with cotton lining.

If you're not at all handy, ask a friend to do your
manicure and return the favor. If you're great at
setting hair or sewing, maybe you can arrange a
regular swap.

Stock up on those cheap, disposable plastic gloves.
Once a week, give yourself a "hand facial" by slather-
ing on warmed hand lotion, then donning gloves. Wear
them at least one hour. Remove and rinse your hands.

Henna your hands for super-softness. Add 2 tablespoons of neutral (colorless) henna to 1 tablespoon of vegetable oil. Warm over a low heat. Apply to hands and leave on 15 minutes. Rinse off and feel that baby skin! Neutral henna can be purchased in drug- and health food stores.

Treat hands to a posthousecleaning oatmeal mask. Mix dry oatmeal with an egg white to form a paste. Apply to your hands. Leave on for fifteen minutes, then rinse off with cool, clear water.

Banish telltale onion odors from your hands after cooking by rubbing them with diluted vinegar. Rinse with cool water to finish, and apply moisturizer.

Fade unsightly tobacco stains from your nails by saturating a cotton ball with lemon juice and rubbing over the stain. If you have no success, rub with the outer peel of the lemon.

Cold cream is a wonderful cuticle softener. Rub it in, then soak your fingers in warm, soapy water and push cuticles back with an orange stick.

Conditioning nail dip: Blend 1 avocado with a tablespoon of vegetable oil. Dip your nails into the puree for 10 minutes, then rinse and buff.

Before swimming in salt or chlorinated water, protect your cuticles with petroleum jelly. Rub in with your finger.

Shake your hands from the wrists—hard—for two or three minutes. This is a naturally relaxing exercise which gets your circulation going.

To massage fingers, start at the base of the finger, and, with firm, back-and-forth motions, work your way out to the fingertips. Use a hand cream for lubrication. Remember, the muscles of your hands work very hard for you. Treat them kindly. Relax them.

Prevent nail breakage and dirt buildup while gardening by first digging nails into a cake of ordinary soap. The soap will support your nails and keep them clean.

Practice picking things up with the cushions of your fingers and not your nails to avoid splitting.

Nails will be less likely to tear if you unfasten difficult jewelry clasps with a metal nail file.

When you sew or embroider, wear a thimble to prevent sore fingers and chipped nail polish.

Keep hand cream by the kitchen sink, and use it after your hands have been in detergents. Prevent rough skin by putting a bottle on your laundry room shelf, too.

Unlined rubber gloves sometimes promote chapping because they keep hands moist and confined. Wear a pair of cotton gloves inside rubber gloves that are a size too big for you.

Do your palms sweat when you're nervous? On occasions when you feel uptight, spray your palms lightly with aerosol antiperspirant.

Clip toenails straight across to prevent ingrowns. Use a cuticle scissors only for snipping off the cuticles that are very long—don't dig in and cut any skin.

Make toe painting easier: Separate toes with toilet tissue. Weave one long piece in and out, or wad little pieces between your toes. Or stand pencils up between your toes.

If you adore very high heels, do extra exercises to strengthen the stomach and back muscles (see pages 186–187). Also, do a calf-stretching workout (page 181) to counteract the shortening effect of your spikes.

Fresh air is good for the feet. So is sun. Air your feet each day to discourage infections that develop when the climate is moist and dark—like in your shoes.

To avoid foot odor, faithfully scrub your feet morning and night in warm, soapy water.

A pumice stone works even better if you wet it before using. Rub over a bar of soap, then circle over heels, callouses and corns.

Avoid athlete's foot by wearing rubber thongs or plastic shoes at the public pool in summer—don't go barefoot. Keep your feet well ventilated, and change your shoes every day so each pair has a chance to dry out completely before being worn again.

An old-fashioned and ever effective foot soak is ½ cup Epsom salts mixed in 2 quarts of warm water. Soak feet for 15 minutes. Pat dry with a soft towel and douse with witch hazel for a cool finish.

Feet will tingle in a soak to which you've added rosemary tea. Boil 1 quart of water and steep 5 tablespoons of dried rosemary. Strain and pour the liquid into a gallon of warm water. Soak feet 20 minutes.

Overnight recipe for baby-soft feet: Massage them with Vaseline, put on a pair of cotton socks and say good night. In the morning, rinse with water and powder with talc.

Relieve foot tension by rolling your arches over a rolling pin. Roll from toes to heel and back, and forth, and back . . . do it five minutes for each foot.

Pick up pebbles with your toes. Do this exercise on

the beach in summer, and in the winter, switch to picking up Junior's marbles from the rug.

Here's a weird-sounding foot massage so terrific you won't believe it until you try it. Into a pair of low-heeled walking shoes pour dried whole peas or beans. Cover the soles. Now put on socks, then the shoes and take a long walk. One of the most ingenious ways to untense those tootsies!

Catch corns, callouses and bunions early. Use simple remedies like scrapers, plasters and medicated discs that can be bought in any drugstore. Don't wait for these simple problems to get serious.

Switch your shoes every day. Switch your heel heights, too. Wearing the same shoes constantly sometimes causes tiny, spidery veins on the legs.

Very high arches will feel extra comfy in a flexible shoe that lets the arch move. Look for a soft rubber sole.

Flat-footed? Wear clogs as often as you can. The firm arch will give you the support your feet need. If you don't like clogs, substitute any supportive leather shoe.

Get exercise sandals with a molded wooden sole. Your feet get a much needed workout every time you wear them, since toes have to grip that rounded ridge under them.

Buy shoes late in the afternoon when your feet are biggest—remember, they swell during the day. Shoes bought before your morning coffee may end up pinching by lunch.

For walking or street wear, don't wear heels more than two inches high—lower is better. Very high heels don't allow the proper walking gait and frequently throw the spine off balance.

Try *both* shoes on before buying. Since your feet are slightly different sizes, make sure the left *and* the right shoes fit well.

Cross your legs at the ankles, not at your knees. Besides being more flattering, the pose is healthier for circulation. Crossing the knees promotes varicose veins.

Chapter 11
Eating for Fitness

What we eat, how we eat and when we eat profoundly affect our health. As the nutrition scientists probe ever deeper the complex relationships between food and fitness, that old cliché, "you are what you eat," gains increasing respectability. Too much of any one type of food can be harmful and can lead to obesity and poor health. Balancing your diet is the key, but you don't have to be a gourmet cook to prepare nutritious meals. It may take a little rearranging of some old habits, but that's the hardest part. "Fitness eating," with its emphasis on crunchy vegetables, sweet fruit, darkly aromatic breads and elegantly lean meat, poultry and fish, can become a fun project for you and your family to explore together.

Add zest to vegetables. On fresh fruit or tossed salads, sprinkle grated orange peel as a tangy topping. If you grate too much, store the extra in a plastic bag in your freezer.

Drink plenty of water—at least six glasses a day. Water is the natural purifier that keeps your system cleansed. Tap water is just fine, but once in a while indulge yourself with bottled spring water. Each spring gives forth water with a unique taste.

Mix fresh fruit with yogurt. Plump blueberries or

juicy strawberries or ripe pineapple and plain yogurt not only tastes better than commercial fruit yogurt, it's lower in calories, too.

Sprinkle raw wheat germ over your breakfast cereal. Wheat germ is full of B vitamins and vitamin E. It's a great extender for hamburgers and meat loaf and adds crunch to salads and yogurt.

Cut down to two beef meals a week. Beef is fairly high in saturated fat, which ups the cholesterol in your blood and spells danger for your heart. Substitute fish, poultry or egg dishes for beef.

Eat potato skins. Some vitamins are concentrated in the outer layers of potatoes, turnips, apples and lemons, among other "skin foods." Don't discard skins, but cultivate a taste for the rougher part of the fruit or vegetable.

Don't salt your food. Instead, learn to use herbs, spices, lemon, lime and onion for seasoning. Limit your salt intake to a teaspoon a day over and above what's naturally contained in your food.

Sweeten tea naturally with a squeeze of fresh orange.

More than three cups of coffee a day may be too much stimulation for some systems. Drink herbal teas instead, especially if you are very nervous. Caffeine may be the culprit.

Eat eggs at least three times a week. Eggs are an excellent source of protein. Adults should have four eggs weekly; children, seven eggs.

Megadoses of vitamins A and D may be toxic. Limit your supplements to one multivitamin daily, unless your doctor recommends otherwise.

Scrub fruits and vegetables to remove superficial chemicals. Use a soft scrubber and soap and water, and be sure to rinse very well.

Squeeze a lemon into tomato or vegetable juice or fruit-based beverages. This natural refresher adds tiny amounts of vitamin C.

Use honey when you can. Honey contains calories, yes, but it also contains small amounts of minerals which white sugar lacks.

Buy mineral water instead of soda. You can make your own "soda" by adding sparkling mineral water to grape juice, orange juice or lemonade.

In July and August, add skim milk, bananas, oranges and apples to your diet to replace minerals and salts lost through perspiration. Dried fruit and nut snacks are good replenishers, too.

Substitute cottage cheese for hard cheese. When you can, choose cottage, farmer, pot or ricotta cheeses, which are lower in fat than harder cheeses.

Have a bran cereal for breakfast if irregularity is a problem. Or sprinkle raw bran over any prepared breakfast cereal. Bran is available in health food stores and any market.

Sip a glass of carrot juice to revive a sluggish digestive system.

Sharpen kitchen knives. If you rip and tear vegetables, more nutrients are lost. Always slice cleanly.

Don't store vegetables and fruits for too long. The sooner you eat them, the more vitamins you reap. Buy only enough for two or three days.

Buy juice-packed fruit. Syrup from packing peaches, pears, cherries and pineapple contains no nutrients except calories; juices contain the nutrients of the fruit.

Use the cooking broth from vegetables to cook rice. Another idea is to store the liquid in the refrigerator and use it to extend tomato or vegetable juice. It's too vitamin-rich to throw out. Use within 2–3 days.

Hot, spicy foods will warm your body in winter. Hot chili, spicy curried beef or peppery Chinese food make your digestive tract feel warm.

Serve fruit with cheese for dessert. Some complementary flavors are apples with Roquefort, pears with Stilton and pineapple with Camembert.

Grow sprouts for salads. Sprouts are rich in vitamins and minerals. They're also an inexpensive salad ingredient. You can purchase alfalfa, mung beans or soybeans at a health food store, Chinese market or your local supermarket. Soak about ½ cup of seeds in water overnight. The next morning, put the seeds in a glass jar or bowl. Cover with a cheesecloth. Twice a day, rinse them with fresh water and drain well through the cloth. The seeds should not be soggy. When the sprouts are about ½" long, harvest them. They can be tossed into any green salad or steamed as you would cook any vegetable.

Basil is easy to grow in a window pot. Cultivate a small crop and use the fresh leaves in salads. With sliced raw tomatoes and a little chopped onion, basil makes a pungent salad. It tastes a bit like mint, the herb family to which it belongs.

Stock up on peanut butter, a rich protein source. You can substitute two tablespoons of peanut butter for a half serving of meat (adults, remember, need two meat group servings daily). Only don't overdo it—unfortunately, peanut butter is rather high in fat.

A bowl of lentil or pea soup is a healthful wintertime lunch. Bean soups are good sources of iron, which is especially important for women. Have a small salad as an accompaniment.

Broil liver with mushroom and onions. Liver is such an outstanding source of iron and vitamins, you really should cultivate a taste for it. Another cooking method is sautéeing—equally delicious.

Plan meals with eye appeal. A slice of red tomato, a sprig of parsley or a spoonful of corn relish will add excitement to a plate. Create a variety of colors and textures, like a picture inside a frame.

Quick-cook your vegetables. Overboiling cooks out their vitamins and sometimes causes undesirable flavors to develop. Vegetables should be crunchy when you bite into them, not soggy.

Fast for one day to cleanse an overworked digestive system. Drink only water or juices, and don't do anything too strenuous. From time to time, your body deserves a rest from its daily labors.

Eat that parsley on your fish. Parsley is ultra high

in vitamin A and also works as an effective breath cleanser after onions and garlic.

Snack on high-protein foods, not sugar snacks. Appease your appetite with a hard-boiled egg, nuts, cold chicken or cheese. Break the habit of sodas, cake and candy for nibbling.

Wholesome pick-me-up: Mix 1 tablespoon of honey and 1 tablespoon of cider vinegar in a glass of water. Drink immediately.

Take a Chinese cooking class. You'll learn a healthful new way to cook and eat, since Chinese cuisine is low in red meat and heavy on vegetables. The wok cooking method insures that food will retain practically all its nutrients.

For a poor skin, add fresh carrots, spinach and sweet potatoes to your diet. These foods contain lots of vitamin A—the good-skin vitamin.

Don't let leftovers sit in the fridge. Eat them within a day or two of cooking. The longer cooked food is kept, the greater the loss in food value. Cooked vegetables, for instance, lose about one-fourth their vitamin C after a day.

Eat coleslaw during flu season. Fresh raw cabbage has plenty of vitamin C, which is important if you can't get the car out of the driveway to go marketing because of snow!

Utilize the stewing juices from meat and poultry in a nourishing soup. The stock is rich in B vitamins.

Substitute skim milk for whole—it contains the other important nutrients but lacks the butterfat.

Brew a "tisane" pick-me-up. Tisane is the French name for those wonderful herbal infusions that make such aromatic teas. Rose hips or linden flowers are two special flavors; prepare them just as you would ordinary tea. The herbs are sold loose (so you will need a teapot) or in tea bags you can steep right in the cup. Check specialty stores for a dazzling array of herbal teas and blends.

Need a new frying pan? A cast-iron skillet has a built-in bonus; it sloughs off some of its iron into your food. Most women can benefit by the extra mineral supplement.

In restaurants, order whole wheat bread. Whole grains have higher quality protein than white bread.

Certain medications don't mix with certain foods and drinks. Ask your druggist or doctor about what to avoid for the duration of your medication.

Going to a party where you'll dine late? Have a small meal early in the evening before you leave. Cottage cheese, fruit, crackers and a glass of milk make a good choice. A snack-dinner will tide you over and prevent you from feeling the dizzying effects of cocktails on an empty stomach.

Salt your food at the *end* of cooking time. Salt draws the juices from meats. Those liquids, besides being tasty, are full of valuable nutrients you don't want to lose.

Take vitamin pills after eating, not before. They need food present in the stomach to work effectively.

Carry sunflower seeds and raisins in your purse. Having your private, nutritious snacks on hand will discourage the pie-and-coffee habit that's delicious but terrible for your figure.

If you're always tired, depressed and not hungry, it may be psychological . . . or your diet may lack thiamine. Eat more lean pork, dried beans and peas. Try a dinner of pea soup and pork chops. Of course, if the situation persists, you should consult a doctor.

Enjoy a baked potato. Potatoes have a terrible reputation, and undeservedly so. They are high in B vitamins, fat free and relatively low in calories—only ninety for one baked in its skin.

Steam your vegetables. Buy an inexpensive steamer or improvise with a colander set over a pot of boiling water. Cover while steaming.

Take a "bouillon break." Bouillon is more nutritious than coffee and won't leave you with the jitters. And if you work, keep a mug and an immersible water heater in your desk to prepare your hot snack.

Eat the outer leaves of lettuce and cabbage. Though not so pretty as the inner leaves, they contain more vitamins.

Cook those carrots! Steam, then serve with a pat of butter and a sprinkling of nutmeg.

Put an apple in your lunchbox. From sweet Delicious to tart Granny Smith, there are varieties to please every palate. An apple is a natural toothbrush.

Subsitute spinach, kale and escarole for iceberg lettuce in salads. Iceberg is crunchy, but not as nutritious as other leafy greens that provide more minerals and vitamins.

Stock up on canned fish. Tuna, salmon and sardines are terrific protein sources. Serve them in new ways—flaked into a luncheon salad, grilled on toast or as croquettes for supper.

Serve brown rice instead of white. Brown rice has slightly more nutritional value than white. If you do buy white rice, make sure it's "enriched."

Serve crudités to your company. These healthful appetizers are fresh, crisp, chilled vegetables, cut into bite-size pieces. Set out a bowl of broccoli florets, carrot sticks, cherry tomatoes, cucumber spears, radishes and cauliflower tops. Serve with a yogurt and dried onion dip.

Avoid the yogurt-for-lunch syndrome. It isn't enough to keep you going all day long. Yogurt is great for a day or two, to lose an odd few pounds, but not as a steady diet.

Avoid cooking with fat. Bake, boil, broil, roast or stew your foods, and fry only infrequently. When you do sauté or pan-fry, use a polyunsaturated oil.

Eat a papaya. This lush, fragrant tropical fruit contains enzymes that aid digestion. If you prefer, drink a glass of papaya juice.

Have a fruit shake before bedtime. Into your blender put 1 cup skim milk, ½ cup fruit (peaches, bananas, strawberries or blueberries), 3 ice cubes and sugar or honey to taste. Blend 30 seconds and drink immediately. This is a fine before-bed snack, since the calcium in the milk will relax your body.

Serve cold vegetable soups in summer. All it takes is your favorite puréed vegetable, chicken stock, cream or milk, salt, pepper and parsley. They are healthful and refreshing accompaniments to sandwiches or salads.

Chew every mouthful of food at least five times. Of course, you can't make rules like that. The point is, don't gulp food down without chewing it. Eat slowly, drawing out every bit of flavor.

Don't buy sweetened breakfast cereals. Neither teeth nor tummy need the sugar. Top an unsweetened cereal with sliced fresh fruit for natural sweetness.

Chapter 12

Sensational Diet Ideas

Losing weight is never, ever easy—and don't let anyone tell you it is. Whether you frame your resolutions with a low-calorie diet, a low-carbohydrate plan or some other medically approved diet, taking off the excess poundage, your own lovable fat, is always hard work. You need all the help you can get. We hope you find some in this chapter.

With more than ten pounds to lose, break your diet up into five-pound mini diets. Plan, for example, to lose five pounds the first month, five pounds the second and so on. This way, the project will seem feasible.

Appease your ravenous appetite with a glass of water thirty minutes before each meal.

Chew food slowly. If you cut everything into ultra-tiny pieces and chew each bite six times, your meal will last longer. And you'll start learning to appreciate the taste of food.

Is a lack of food making you frustrated? Bang the bed! Take an old tennis racket and whack the mattress hard when you've reached your emotional limit. Keep hitting until you feel better—you will. If you don't own a racket, pummel with your fists.

Calculate your calorie needs by multiplying your "desirable weight" by fifteen if you are sedentary and by twenty if you are active. Take in just this number of calories daily to keep your weight stable.

Before starting any diet, telephone your doctor. He may want to see you before you begin.

Eat fruit every day. Reach for a pear instead of a pastry, an apple instead of an apple turnover and cherries instead of chocolate. You'll soon *prefer* the taste of a juicy fruit.

So "no" to seconds if food is served family-style. Use your reserves of willpower to refuse those extra helpings.

Start a diet notebook. Chart your calories in a pocket-size blank book. Write down *everything* (down to chewing gum and coffee!) immediately after you eat it. If you have to list it, you'll think twice about cheating.

Really ravenous? Sip a cup of hot bouillon.

Buy a pretty bathroom scale if your is old or ugly. Splurge on a super-accurate scale that harmonizes with your bathroom decor. This trick will be incentive to step on it.

Whenever you focus on negative thoughts (like "I'm so *fat!*" or "I'll *never* be attractive no matter how much I lose"), consciously switch your mind to a positive thought (like "I lost two pounds this week" or "I think I'll try my hair a new way"). This will require a herculean effort at first, but soon you'll find yourself looking at the bright side automatically.

Instead of snacking when you come home from work, exercise. Bending, stretching, jumping, running —whatever you do—will take the edge off your hunger.

Eat in courses, the French way. Soup first, then salad. Then the main course. Then a pitcher of ice water to clear the palate for dessert and coffee. When you dine so slowly, you'll be content with smaller portions. In fact, you many not even want dessert!

Have a gourmet adventure. Use diet time to test out the many bottled spring and mineral waters— domestic and imported—on the market. Try to discern the taste differences among them.

Organize a "diet watchers" group at work. Bring diet lunches from home and eat together, or just report your weight and progress at a Friday diet meeting. Have one member keep a record of everyone's progress.

Leave a little food over. "Cleaning your plate" may be a holdover habit from childhood and not a true reflection of how hungry you are. It's important to break old patterns that may be causing you to over-eat and gain weight.

Feel the irresistible urge to eat? Leave the house and take a walk. Don't take any money to spend at the local coffee shop!

Use a pocket calculator to count calories. It's easier than pencil and paper. Keep a running count to avoid going over your limit.

On a business lunch? At a party? Order tomato juice with a dash of hot pepper sauce and Worcester-shire, a sprinkling of pepper and a squeeze of lemon. Only about sixty calories for this festive drink!

Slice vegetables in new ways: Julienne carrots into tiny sticks, cut zucchini into chunks, dice greeen beans, slice Brussels sprouts . . . maintain your en-thusiasm by making meal preparation a creative ex-perience.

Purchase mini food storage containers for brown-bag lunches. They're ideal for salad, fruit, cheese, cot-tage cheese and cold meats.

Find a reason for losing weight. Want to get that promotion at work? Want to wow them on the beach this summer? A specific goal will really fire your in-centive to get those pounds off.

Instead of broiling or baking fish with butter, use lemon juice or white wine.

Add ice cubes to any drink, even water. Dieters need special treatment because they feel so deprived. Ice cubes are always festive.

If the scale reports one pound gained, diet it off the next day. One pound is easier to lose than an accumulation of weight. Be sure to weigh yourself at the same time each day for an accurate reading.

If you have over twenty pounds to lose, start dieting with a crash. The instant results will encourage you to keep going. Of course, you should get your doctor's approval if you plan such a drastic diet and follow it for one week only.

Eat small, frequent meals, not two or three giant ones. Snack-eating is psychologically satisfying and healthful, too. Keep to a maximum of 500 calories at each mini meal and don't go over your total daily calorie limit!

Use a nonstick pan for sautéeing or pan frying to cut down on fat.

Trim all fat from your meat before cooking.

Use pretty placemats and napkins. If you make every meal an occasion, your diet will be more fun. You can even drink your water or diet soda from a wine glass.

Buy a bouquet of fresh flowers. After the first rush of interest dies down, dieters frequently get depressed. Fragrant blooms in a vase on your table will lift your spirits.

Substitute skim milk for regular milk or cream in your general cooking. In your coffee, too.

Ask a good friend to phone you every night to check up on your diet—like a diet therapist. You report what you've eaten, what your mood has been and how much you've lost. Don't chat about anything else —save gossip for a separate phone call. At the end of your diet, buy your friend a great present and pay for those phone calls!

Having lunch in a restaurant? Order the fashionable "wine spritzer," which is white wine mixed with club soda or sparkling mineral water. Another cool slimmer is club soda added to orange or grapefruit juice with a wedge of lime, or grenadine mixed into club soda.

Choose water-packed tuna, lower in calories than oil-packed.

Do you really hate to diet? A low-carbohydrate diet will probably work best for you since these plans tend to change the foods you eat radically, and you'll be able to get interested in this aspect of the diet. Also, the rules aren't so strict as with most low-calorie plans.

Do you have a methodical nature? Follow a low-calorie diet. You'll have to count and record calories, measure foods and plan it all out—just the things you like to do.

Drink herbal teas. These noncaffeinated drinks smell wonderful and appease the appetite.

Choose a diet you can live with. Make a list of all the foods you can't bear to give up. Now list those you wouldn't miss. List your eating patterns (at home or out, three full meals or five mini meals). Check any diet you are considering against your lists. See that they match up. If they don't, look for a better diet.

Don't give up if you cheat. Every dieter cheats. Just get back on your regimen and don't fret about the mistake. Use an extra dose of willpower to stay "good."

You'll get more beverage for your calories if you dilute juices and alcoholic drinks with plain water.

Stock carrots, cukes and celery in your refrigerator for low-calorie snacking.

Clam juice, with the smell of the sea in every bottle, is very low in calories. It's a great diet drink.

Remove all skin from chicken before cooking. You'll be cutting away fat and calories.

A 1200-calorie-a-day diet is a safe one for most women. On it, you should shed about two pounds a week.

Take one multivitamin supplement a day when dieting.

Don't diet when you are emotionally upset. If you are quitting smoking, going on vacation, getting married or divorced or changing your job, don't diet. Wait for a stress-free time to begin this very stress-filled project.

Get plenty of sleep when dieting—no less than seven to eight hours a night.

Stick adhesive-backed mirror tiles on your refrigerator door. When you sail into the kitchen for a snack, you'll have to look yourself in the eye.

Avoid wearing loose clothing that allows for easy

expansion. If you wear a form-fitting dress or a blouse and skirt, overeating will make you uncomfortable.

In a restaurant, ask for your salad with lemon wedges, not high-calorie dressing. Another good dressing is oil and vinegar. They usually come in cruets, so you can be lavish with the vinegar and stingy with the oil.

Order a meat dish without gravy and order your vegetables without butter. Ask the waitress for fish to be broiled "dry" with only lemon juice. If the kitchen doesn't adhere to your requests, don't hesitate to send your meal back.

Position a mirror in front of you while you eat. This way you can watch yourself for gobbling. Practice eating slowly—and attractively.

If you're visiting friends, don't hesitate to take along your own diet drink. Not everyone stocks these beverages, so you're better safe than having to break your diet.

At a dinner party, food is frequently lavish. Don't make a big noise about dieting and not being able to eat what's served. Just eat what you can—the meat or fish or chicken and the vegetables or salad. Skip dessert, even if it looks irresistible.

After you've lost your weight, keep tabs on your

figure. Look at your body in the mirror every day. Check the rear view, too, appraising your bottom, midriff and back at full length. Remember, your shape should be great coming and going!

Last-ditch diet tip: Paint your kitchen blue. This super-cool color will tone down your appetite as well as your emotions. Yellow, the traditional kitchen color, is too stimulating for dieters.

Use a tape measure. Check your shrinking proportions every week of your diet and/or exercise program. Write down the numbers in a special notebook. You'll be encouraged by your progress to stay with it.

Have your picture taken "before" you diet. Tack it up on the refrigerator. Need we say more?

Diet with a partner. Suggest the idea to your husband, your friend, your mother—anyone who needs prodding to lose weight. A diet will be easier when you can commiserate with a fellow-sufferer.

Vary your meals. Don't bore yourself into cheating with the same old menus, day in and day out. Try new foods or new ways of preparing the old foods. Really use your cookbooks.

Lose one pound more than what your diet calls for. With this "insurance policy," you won't get too de-

pressed if you overeat on occasion. You can just cut
down the next day.

Resolve every morning that you will stick to your
diet. It is important to recommit yourself to your goal
every single day.

Plan weekends around activities, not eating. It
could be a visit to a friend on Saturday and bike
riding with the family on Sunday. Whatever you do,
plan in advance. Nothing-doing weekends are hazard-
ous for dieters, since it's all too easy to end up by the
refrigerator door.

Beware the third week of your diet—it's when most
dieters quit. By this week, your diet is no longer a
novelty, so you'll be feeling deprived and angry.
Also, the quick weight loss of the first two weeks—
largely water weight—will have tapered off. Muster
all your willpower and force yourself to stay with it.

Redo a room. Now that you are taking better care
of how you look, take pride in your surroundings, too.
Painting a room, wallpapering a bathroom or sewing
new throw pillows for a couch will keep you so busy
you won't have time to think about food.

Forsake french fries. You'll be amazed at how often
you really do eat them once you have to give them up.

Stay out of the kitchen. The kitchen table is a cozy place for sitting, chatting, writing letters, sewing, paying bills . . . but it keeps you near food. Learn to utilize other places in your house and confine time in the kitchen to food preparation and/or dining.

Chapter 13

Best
Exercises
Ever

Exercise we must! To be truly fit, every woman must pursue some form of physical activity on a regular basis. The effects of aerobic exercises like running, jumping rope or cycling, which give the heart and lungs a workout, benefit the entire body. Other types of exercise concentrate on strengthening our muscles and promoting flexibility. Remember, a beautiful body is a healthy body, and a healthy body is a fit body—less prone to physical and mental disturbances. The first part of this chapter offers general exercise ideas. The second half describes a set of exercises to tone and firm every part of your figure. For these, all you need is a leotard or some comfortably loose clothing and a soft surface to work on. A folded blanket spread on a rug is ideal. At first, do as many repetitions as you can without strain. You may gradually work beyond the suggested repetitions as you become stronger with daily practice.

Practice one aerobic exercise three times a week. It could be running, jumping rope, bicycling, roller skating—any sport that raises your heart rate, gets oxygen racing through your bloodstream and keeps those muscles in action.

Experts recommend aerobic exercise that raises your pulse rate (for giving your heart a workout). To test your pulse: Press the second, third and fourth fingers of one hand against the other wrist. Feel for your pulse. Count the beats for ten seconds. Multiply the number by six for your pulse rate. Check with your doctor before elevating your pulse rate.

Alternate an "aerobic" with a "strength-building" exercise every other day. Calisthenics, fencing and weight lifting are strength and muscle builders. Your body needs both types of workout.

Exercise fifteen minutes a day. This is minimum—thirty minutes is better. Carve out a space in your schedule for workouts six days a week. Take one day off to rest, perhaps Sunday.

Choose an exercise opposite to what you do all day. If you sit behind a desk from nine to five, choose an exercise that is quick and strenuous—squash or running would be good. If you're a full-time mother, racing after kids all day long, choose a calm exercise like yoga or modern dance. If your job requires emotional control, as teaching or law do, an exercise like karate will release your pent-up aggressions. So will fencing. Let your exercise benefit you mentally, too.

Are you naturally tight-jointed? Do more exercises like yoga and stretching that promote flexibility. If you are naturally flexible, do more muscle toners—calisthenics, for instance. *Note*: To discover your flexibility level, try to stretch your thumb back to your wrist. If it reaches to more than a right angle, you're flexible. If not, you're tight.

Tailor your fitness plan to your lifestyle. In other words, don't sign up for a regular dance class if you have little ones and can't always get a baby-sitter. For you, jogging might be better; you can run at your convenience. Give your exercise plan the best chance to succeed.

Vulnerable backs and weak knees raise special problems. Certain exercises may not be safe for you. Check with your doctor.

Exercise gradually. Don't jump in at the advanced level if you haven't moved a muscle in years. Start at the beginner level, work up gradually, then keep at a maintenance level. Resist the impulse to accelerate your training schedule.

Novice runners should alternate running and walking. Run for one minute, then walk for two—a total of fifteen minutes.

Run with your dog. If you're taking Fido out anyway, why not use this time to jog around the block? You'll both be healthier for the exercise.

In bad weather, run in place indoors. Beginning joggers should do seventy-five steps per minute for ten minutes. Intermediates should do seventy-five steps per minute for thirteen minutes. Advanced runners can do seventy-five steps per minute for fifteen minutes. Wear regular running shoes to cushion your feet.

Puncture a big blister with a sterilized needle and let it drain. Cover with an antiseptic cream and a bandage. Leave the bandage on for several days while healing takes place. Meanwhile, continue your running as usual.

Regular joggers, swimmers, skiers, tennis players and aerobic athletes should replace carbohydrates. Don't subsist on a high-protein diet. Latest research shows your body needs those carbohydrates for energy.

Get the full aerobic benefits of walking by following a brisk pace. Swing arms naturally and keep your body relaxed. Don't bounce up and down. Push off your back foot and continue the push all along your foot, down to the big toe.

Walk an hour a day. Make your ultimate goal three miles per hour for overall fitness.

If you can walk, don't drive. Think twice about using your car to go to work, to the drugstore, to a neighbor's house. Once you get in the walking habit, you'll hate using your automobile.

Do you work in an elevator building? Walk up the

stairs to your office. For one week, pretend the elevator hasn't been invented.

Walk barefoot. It's healthful for your feet and great for your legs. Best is going without shoes on grass or sand.

Keep moving on the tennis court. Don't just stand in one spot. Keeping on the go will not only improve your game, it will also increase your aerobic gains!

If you pull a leg muscle or strain your wrist at tennis, don't discontinue all exercise. When the worst of the injury is past, work out everything but the affected part with different types of exercise—calisthenics, for example.

Get your hair out of your eyes. Secure long hair back in a ponytail or braid. Wear a sweat band under your bangs to take them off your forehead. As well as improving your vision, you'll be minimizing the contact of greasy, sweaty hair with your complexion.

Keep cool on the tennis courts by saturating your terry wristband and headband with cool water from the drinking fountain.

If you're plagued with chronic back problems, swim regularly. Swimming is the great all-around exercise. It won't stress your back at all.

Do you have a small bosom? Swimming won't increase the size of your breasts, but it will develop your chest muscles, giving the illusion of a bigger bosom. Concentrate on the crawl, breast and backstrokes— and swim hard.

In the pool, give legs an extra workout—water resistance helps tone muscles. Hold onto the shallow edge. Kick your leg up to the front, to the side, and then to the back. Repeat to both sides.

Want to firm thighs and buttocks? Hang onto a flutterboard and swim back and forth across the pool powered only by the kicking of your legs!

If you're a regular swimmer, wear a comfortable bathing suit that doesn't bind. A sleek style in stretchable fabric is good. Some dance leotards double beautifully as swimsuits.

Going through an emotionally difficult period? Sign up for a dance class. Ballet, folk, modern, jazz, tap all make you feel good. As well as stimulating your body, dancing provides form and structure, the order your life needs right now.

Turn on the radio to a rock or disco station and really let loose! Do all the steps you're too inhibited to do in public. Dance until you're perspiring.

Before you go out dancing, do fifteen minutes of

warmups. Remember, dancing to a frenetic beat is strenuous, just like any other exercise. You risk pulled muscles without warming up.

Practice body balance on a moving bus or subway. Stand with a featherweight hold on the strap. Shift your weight and center of gravity according to the shifts of the vehicle. Hold tight only if you have to.

Keep your bicycle in low gear. You'll get the most exercise benefits from biking if you let your muscles do most of the work.

Get yourself going in the morning by exercising in bed. A few situps, leg lifts and side leg raises will energize you for anything the day has in store.

Exercise in the fresh air. From spring through early fall (or all year round if the climate is mild), do your calisthenics or yoga on the soft grass—a natural exercise mat. If the ground is cool or hard, spread a foam-rubber mat beneath you as you stretch your muscles and aerate your system.

Ankle weights make legs work harder. You'll get quicker results from calisthenics if you use them, but don't wear more than five pounds on each ankle. Heavier weights can strain the spine.

Avoid rubber or plastic exercise suits. They can be

dangerous, since they sometimes cause a rapid and unhealthy loss of the body's stored salt and potassium.

Don't waste TV-watching time. Get down on the floor and do some leg raises, situps, neck rolls and arm circles.

Make your own exercise mat. Buy a piece of foam rubber three feet by six feet. Cover it with cotton or terry fabric or with two beach towels. Stitch along three sides, and close the fourth side with snaps or Velcro for easy laundering.

Exercise studios and local Y's frequently hold early A.M. classes especially for working women. Investigate the possibilities in your community.

Do you have a private office at work? At noon, shut the door, change into a leotard or shorts and do a half hour of stretches and exercises. One extra benefit: You'll feel more awake during the afternoon.

During menstruation, modify your exercise level only if you have severe cramps or a very heavy flow. Otherwise, there's no reason to curtail your workouts. In fact, many doctors feel exercise can lessen the severity of menstrual cramps and abdominal tension.

After vigorous exercise, cool down for fifteen minutes. Keep your body moving slowly. You might take a slow walk or do your pre-exercise warmups again.

Just don't stop exercising suddenly. The shock isn't good for your body.

Wait fifteen minutes after exercising to shower. A shower before then is useless, since your eccrine (sweat) glands take a quarter hour or so to stop their feverish production.

Muscle cramps? Stop exercising, massage the knot or cramp, then slowly stretch the muscle area. Remember, massage, then stretch.

For sports-induced strains and sprains, a cold compress is always a safe treatment. Apply ice wrapped in a washcloth or an ice bag immediately.

Instead of expensive liniment, rub plain camphorated oil into sore muscles for relief:

For sports, wear cotton underwear. Cotton absorbs perspiration. Nylon or synthetic fibers don't, and the continually moist environment encourages infections and rashes.

"Sports bras" are especially designed for strenuous activity. Buy one to avoid chafing and discomfort. If you are large-breasted, the extra support is especially important.

Dress for the weather when you are doing strenuous

exercise outdoors. Wear a sweatsuit when it gets cool. In winter, don thermal underwear under the suit and a windbreaker over it. A wool cap helps retain body heat. To prevent chilling, wrap a scarf around your neck.

Looking for a light, pre-sport meal that's high in energy? Blend 1 cup skim milk, 1 teaspoon honey, 1 raw egg, 3 fresh strawberries, ½ banana, 2 tablespoons protein powder (sold in health food stores) and 3 ice cubes. Blend at high speed and drink immediately.

Potassium depletion can be prevented by sipping orange juice and eating a banana every day. Peanuts, sunflower seeds and pistachio nuts are other good sources of potassium, an essential body salt released by the body in perspiration.

In hot weather, drink plenty of water and juices to avoid dehydration.

Before a marathon or tennis match, have a light, balanced meal that's high in carbohydrates—like spaghetti and meatballs. Don't overload on proteins or fat. Eat about three hours before the event to allow enough time for digestion.

Stand when you talk on the phone. Moving around will keep your muscles warm and help guard against fanny spread.

Here's a great chair exercise: Spread your knees apart and drop your head and arms between them. Relax five seconds. Slowly return to an upright seated position. This will stretch your spine and relax your body.

Standing at the stove over a long dinner preparation? Lift one foot and make a circle with your ankle, then reverse and circle around the other way. Repeat with your other foot. Doing this will prevent pins and needles by keeping your circulation alive.

Keep a straight spine when doing housework.

Use dishwashing time to strengthen leg muscles. Rise up on your toes, then lower your heels. Repeat.

Do housework quickly and energetically, and you'll burn up lots of calories. Think of chores in terms of exercise.

How about storing your laundry and cleaning supplies in the attic or basement? You'll have to run up and down the stairs to get them whenever you want to clean!

Use vacuuming time to work out your legs. Push the vacuum forward by bending one knee deeply in a fencer's lunge. Then straighten the leg, and next time you push the vacuum, bend the other knee.

Practice a dancer's posture: Stand with your back to a wall and press your head, shoulders and spine flat against it. Now walk away from the wall. Try to maintain the posture achieved.

Fight against slumped shoulders by extending your arms in front of you. Now swing them back in wide circles—as big as you can make them. Reverse direction and circle arms from back to front, in almost a swimming motion.

Help yourself stand straight and walk tall: Place your fingers at the back of your neck and make circles with your elbows. Circle back and front to relax your shoulders and unkink the knots in your upper back.

When you take your car to town, park three or four blocks from your final destination. Make yourself walk that extra distance for the exercise. Remember, all those little distances add up.

Invisible bus stop exercise: Grip the buttocks together tightly, pushing your pelvis forward and keeping your knees straight. Now relax your buttocks. Now grip them tight, and relax . . . you should feel those underused muscles really working!

Invisible desk exercise. Pull your stomach muscles in as tightly as possible—keep your diaphragm pulled in, too. Now relax the muscles. Now pull in again . . . and relax.

Wonderful Warmups

Side Bender (for the waist and sides): Stand with your feet shoulder-width apart, hands on waist. Slowly bend to your left side. Feel the stretch all along the right side. Hold for five seconds. Now bend to the right. Repeat five times to each side.

Floor Stretcher (for the thighs and spine): Sit on the floor with your legs wide apart. Bend over from the waist and reach forward as far as you can. Hold for fifteen seconds. Repeat five times.

Calf Stretcher (for the lower legs): Stand about three feet from a wall with your palms on it at shoulder level. With your back straight and heels on the floor, lean in toward the wall. Bend your elbows and push your pelvis forward. Hold for thirty seconds. Repeat five times.

Sports Stretch (for the whole body): Sit with your right leg in front of you and your left leg bent in close to the body. Your left thigh should be at a right angle to your body. Gently stretch forward. Try to touch the right foot with your left hand. Hold for twenty seconds. Repeat three times with each leg.

Jumping Jacks (for the entire body): Stand with feet apart, your arms down at your sides. Jump, bringing your feet together and clapping your hands overhead simultaneously. Now jump apart and bring your arms down to your sides. Maintain a quick rhythm and repeat twenty times.

For Lovely Hands

Two-Fister (for the wrists and top of hands): Extend your arms straight in front of you. Make two fists. Slowly circle them right, ten times. Now circle them left, also ten times. Repeat the sequence again.

All-Hand Stretch (for the fingers and joints): Place the tips of your fingers on the edge of a table. Push your hand down so you feel the stretch all along your fingers, then bounce it gently against the table. Stretch your thumb separately against the table. Repeat with the other hand.

Pianist's Exercise (for the fingers): Curve your fingers down on a table, as if playing the piano. Lift each finger separately ten times, as high as possible, keeping all the others touching the table. Repeat with the other hand.

Ten-Finger Stretch (for the fingers): Hold both hands up in front of you. Stretch your fingers as far apart as possible. Hold ten seconds. Release. Repeat five times.

The Squeeze (for the entire hand): Grab a child's rubber ball and squeeze it tight for ten seconds. Release. Repeat five times with each hand.

For a Fine Throat

Yoga Neck Stretch (for the neck): Sit at a table. Clasp your hands behind your neck and place your elbows on the table. Turn your head to the right and rest your chin in the right palm (left hand is at back of neck). Gently turn your head right, as far as you can. Return your head slowly. Now repeat to the left, resting your chin in the left palm this time. Repeat the entire sequence five times.

Throat Firmer (for the chin and throat): Sit with your legs front, your hands behind the buttocks. Lift your chest high and let your head fall back as far as possible. Be sure to keep your mouth closed. Hold for ten seconds and raise your head slowly to the starting position. Repeat five times.

Head Circles (for the neck): Drop your head onto your chest. Roll it to the right, then back, then left, then down to your chest again. Reverse the direction. Keep your shoulders down as you roll your head. Repeat five times in each direction.

Model's Walk (for correct position of the neck and chin): Stand tall and balance a heavy, hardcover book on your head. With your chin up, walk around the room for two minutes.

Chin Toner (for the neck): Lie on your bed on your back. Let your head hang off the edge. Lift your head up and try to touch your chest with your chin. Now let your head drop back again. Repeat three times.

For Shapely Arms and Bosom

Palm Press (for the chest muscles): Stand with your feet together. Interlock the fingers of both hands at chest level, with your elbows out to the side. Push your palms together with all your strength. Relax. Repeat five times.

Shoulder Relaxer (for the upper body): Stand with your hands at your sides. Now clasp your hands behind you with palms facing and fingers interlocked. Raise your arms as high as possible in back, keeping them straight. Bounce them up three times, then return to your original position. Repeat five times.

The Windmill (for the arms and shoulders): Stand erect with your arms at your sides. Bring your right arm up and move it back in a wide circle. When your arm is circling to the back, lift your left arm up in front and begin to circle back with it. Both arms should swing around simultaneously—like a windmill. Repeat for thirty seconds.

The Fling (for the upper arms): Stand with your body erect, arms extended in front of you at shoulder level. Palms should be touching. Fling your arms back as far as possible, keeping them at shoulder level. Bring them front again. Keep a straight torso. Repeat ten times.

Classic Pushup (for arms and chest): Lean on your hands and feet, with your body straight from head to heels. Keeping your spine straight, bend your elbows and lower your body to the floor. Now straighten your elbows. Repeat five times. *Note*: If this push is too difficult, begin with the modified version. It's done in exactly the same way, except you begin by resting on your hands and *knees*, with your knees together and hands shoulder-width apart. If you start out with the easier pushup, you'll gradually build up the strength in your arms and torso, then you can move on to the tougher version.

For a Willowy Waist

Torso Twister (for the waist): Stand with your feet apart, hands on your waist. Twist as far to the right as you can. Now twist to the left. Repeat the sequence ten times.

The Back Stretch (for the side and spine muscles): Stand with your feet shoulder-width apart. Clasp hands behind your neck. Bend back from the waist, as far as you can without losing your balance. Return to the starting position. Now bend back and to the right. Return to the starting position. Bend back and to the left. Return. Repeat the sequence three times.

Side Touches (for the waist and trunk): Stand with your feet apart. Arms are overhead. Twist to the left and bend down over your left leg. Stand up and repeat to the right side. Repeat the sequence eight times.

Sitover Stretch (for the waist and legs): Sit with your legs extended in front, arms up overhead. Bend over from the hips. Reach for your toes with your fingers and try to touch your forehead to your knees. If you can't, get your head down as far as possible. Hold five seconds, then sit up again. Repeat five times.

The Upper Body Arch (for the waist and torso): Lie on your stomach. Bend your legs and grasp the ankles. Keep your thighs apart. Pull your torso up as high as possible and look up at the ceiling. Hold for ten seconds, then relax. Repeat three times.

For a Trim Tummy

The Roll (for the abdomen): Lie on your back with your arms at your sides. Slowly roll up to a 45° angle by first raising the head and shoulders, then raising your arms forward. Next, pull in your abdominal muscles and contract the buttocks tight. Hold this position—halfway up to sitting—for ten seconds, then slowly uncurl your body back to the floor, reversing the steps, one by one. Repeat three times.

Alternate Toe Touch (for the abdomen and spine): Lie on your back, arms at your sides. Raise one leg and touch your toes with the opposite hand. Lift your head and shoulders a bit. Relax your body to the floor and repeat with the other leg. Repeat the sequence eight times.

Bent-Knee Situp (for the abdomen): Lie on your back, with fingers clasped behind your neck and your knees bent. In one movement, sit up and bring your elbows forward. Slowly uncurl your body to the floor. Repeat five times.

The Backbend (for the abdomen and spine): Sit on your heels, arms at your sides. Slowly inch your hands back to about a foot behind you and rest on your palms. Drop your head back and raise your chest.

Arch your back in a backbend. Hold for ten seconds and slowly return to the starting position.

Tummy Toner (for the abdomen and legs): Lie flat on the floor, arms at your sides. Bend your knees and raise them up to your chest. Point your toes and raise your legs to the ceiling. Pulling those stomach muscles in tightly, slowly lower your legs to the floor. Repeat five times.

For Slimmer Hips

Pelvic Press (for the hips and buttocks): Lie on your back, knees bent, arms about fifteen inches from your body, palms to the floor. Tighten your stomach muscles, squeeze your buttocks together and press the small of your back against the floor. Now, tilt the pelvis up, as you try to keep every inch of your spine glued to the floor! Release and repeat five times.

Hip Roll (for the hips): Lie on the floor, arms out to the sides, and palms down. Bend your knees up to your chest. Keeping them together and touching, roll your knees to the right side and touch the floor. Now roll your knees to the left. Keep those shoulders pressed to the floor—don't lift them off! Repeat the sequence five times.

Fanny Walk (for the hips, buttocks and legs): Sit with your legs out in front of you, arms extended straight ahead. Keep your back erect. Begin "walking" by lifting one hip and pushing it forward. Put it down. Lift the other hip and push *it* forward. Put it down. Continue "walking" across the room, then reverse direction and walk "backwards" to where you started. Keep this up for two full minutes.

The Pullup (for the hips and thighs): Stand with your legs together, arms at your sides. Raise the right knee up to your chest and clasp your hands around it. Pull the knee in and up as far as you can. Lower your leg. Repeat with your left knee. Repeat the sequence five times.

The Hipster (for the hips and buttocks): Lie on your left side, with your arm bent and your head resting on your left palm. The left knee is bent in at a right angle to the body. Bend your right knee and bring it up toward your chest. Now extend the leg straight down (following the line of your body). Keep it parallel to the floor but not touching. Repeat this sequence—it's a pulleylike movement—fifteen times. Then repeat with the other leg.

Yoga Lift (for the hips and lower back): Lie on your stomach, with your arms folded and your chin resting on the hands. Legs are together. Raise your right leg as high as you can without lifting your right pelvic bone off the floor. Hold high in the air fifteen seconds. Return it to the floor. Repeat with the left leg. Repeat the sequence five times.

For Supple Spine

Seated Curl (for the spine): Sit erect with your legs crossed. Rest your palms on your knees. Slowly drop your chin, lower your head and round the spine. Get your head as close to the floor as you can. Bounce gently five times. Uncurl your spine slowly and return to the starting position. Repeat five times.

Knee Pull (for the lower back): Lie on your back, with your knees bent and feet flat on the floor. Grasp your left knee with both hands and pull it up to your chest, as close as possible. Return it to the starting position. Now straighten the same leg up to the ceiling. Return it to the original position. Repeat with the right leg. Repeat the entire sequence five times.

Seated Arch (for the spine): Sit on the floor with your feet toegther and legs extended in front. Grasp your ankles with both hands and slowly let your body drop forward. Touch your head to your knees (or get it as close as you can). Now, inhale slowly and as you do, arch your spine and look up—remember, you're still holding onto those ankles! Hold for five seconds and relax, rounding your back again. Repeat three times.

Overhead Swing (for the whole back): Lie flat on your back, with legs separated slightly. Arms are overhead and palms up. Raise your legs and swing them back over your head until your toes touch the floor behind you. Slowly uncurl your body to the floor, reversing the steps. *Note*: The movement should be smooth.

For Streamlined Thighs

Killer Thigh Raise (for the outer thighs and buttocks): Kneel on all fours. Keep your back straight.

Raise your right leg to the right side about twelve inches from the floor. Now kick your leg up even higher. Bounce it up and down eight times and return your leg to the floor. Repeat five times to each side.

Kneel Back (for the front of thighs): Kneel with your legs slightly apart, arms raised in front. Keeping your back straight, lean your body back slowly, as far as you can without straining. Hold for ten seconds. Pull yourself back up to the starting position. Repeat three times.

Fencer's Lunge (for the entire thigh): Stand with your hands on your hips, feet apart and right foot pointing to the right. Bend your right knee and lean to the right, shifting all your weight onto your right leg. Swing back to the original position. Repeat with the left leg. Repeat the sequence eight times.

Ballet Bend (for the thighs and calves): Stand erect and hold onto the back of a chair with one hand for balance. Rise up on your toes. Slowly bend your knees and lower your body all the way down in a deep knee bend, keeping your heels off the floor. Rise up again slowly, straightening your legs. Don't let those heels touch the ground! Repeat five times.

Isometric Press (for the inner thighs): Lie on your back with your knees bent and your heels on the floor. Place a child's rubber ball between your knees and press them together as hard as you can. Hold for ten seconds, then relax. Repeat five times.

For Limber Legs

Leg Pulser (for the entire leg): Lie on your back with your knees bent and heels on the floor. Extend your right leg up and flex the foot. Grasp the leg behind the knee and pulse it up toward your chest. Point the foot, bend the knee and return your leg to the starting position. Repeat with the other leg. Repeat the sequence five times.

Athlete's Switch (for the entire leg): Place your hands on the floor, about shoulder-width apart. Bend your right knee up to your chest under you. Your left leg is straight out behind. In one jump, switch legs so that now your left knee is bent up to your chest and your right leg is stretched out in back. Repeat ten times.

Ballet Kicks (for the entire leg): Stand with your legs together. With one hand, hold onto a chair for balance, your side facing the chair. Kick your right leg up in front, as high as possible. Now kick out to the side. Now kick up in back. Repeat sequence five times, then switch sides and repeat with the other leg.

The Bicycle (for the legs and spine): Lie on your back. Bend your knees and lift your back off the floor. Support your back with your hands. Straighten your legs overhead and begin to pedal as you would a bike.

Pedal quickly, without stopping, for one full minute, then uncurl your body back to the starting position.

Side Leg Raises (for the outer legs): Lie on your side, one arm propping your head, the other palm on the floor for support. Raise the top leg as high as you can without bending it. Now lower it. Repeat ten times with each leg.

For Fabulous Feet

Ankle Unwinder (for the ankles): Sit on the floor with your legs extended in front of you, spine straight. Position palms behind your buttocks. Circle your feet outward in opposing circles, ten times. Reverse direction, rotating your feet in inward circles, ten times. Repeat the entire sequence.

Foot Flexer (for ankles and shins): Sit on the floor, your legs in front of you and palms behind buttocks. Extend your feet with the toes pointed. Now flex your feet, pointing your toes up to the ceiling. Repeat fifteen times.

Toe Clench (for the toes): Sit with your legs in front of you, resting your palms behind your buttocks. Curl the toes of your left foot and clench them tightly. Now release and spread your toes as far apart as possible. Repeat ten times with each foot.

Pencil Pick-up (for the toes' agility): Stand in your bare feet. With the toes of one foot, pick up a pencil

from the floor. Drop it. Repeat five times with each
foot.

Yoga De-Tenser (for your toes): Sit with your
knees together, legs bent under you. Flex your feet so
the toes are on the floor and you are sitting on your
heels. Bounce very gently ten times.

Chapter 14

More Energy,
Sounder Sleep

Women today lead rewarding, yet complicated lives. Most of us between the ages of eighteen and forty-five are employed, and many women hold down two demanding jobs—a career and a full-time job as homemaker and mother. It can be a stressful way to live if we fail to channel our energies wisely. Learning how to relax is especially important. This chapter will teach you some good ways to banish tension, have more energy and enjoy a good night's sleep.

Take three very deep breaths. Inhale, letting the air expand your diaphragm and abdomen, like a big balloon. Hold for five seconds, then exhale slowly, forcing every drop of air out of your body. You'll feel peppier with more oxygen in your system.

When your body feels tired, give it rest. Either go to sleep early or take a short nap. Learn to listen to the messages your body sends out all the time.

Refuel with a tea break. Into a cup of tea pour the juice of one fresh-squeezed orange. Add one teaspoon of honey and sip.

Chronic fatigue may mean you're bored. Do one

new thing, something you've never done but always wished to do. It could be something small, like buying yourself flowers, saying "good morning" to an attractive man in your office or starting a new book or sewing project.

Banish mid-morning slumps with ten deep breaths, ten jumping jacks and ten deep knee bends.

Big night on the town? Draw the blinds, slip between the covers and sleep for two hours before dressing. That nap will energize you and do more than makeup to help you look sensational!

If you're an expert at yoga, do a headstand. Take the phone off the hook and do one freestanding, or support yourself against a wall. With a fresh blood supply to your head, you'll feel more alert right away.

Sing in the shower. Sing anywhere, for that matter. Singing draws lots of oxygen into the body, and that translates into more energy as it's utilized by your system.

Stand with your legs apart. Bend over from the waist, letting your head and arms hang totally relaxed. Swing from right to left, from left to right, and and again and again for thirty seconds—really sway! Slowly uncurl back to a standing position.

Tired feet? Revive them by sitting on the edge of

your tub and letting alternate blasts of hot and cold water shower over your ankles and toes.

An instant waker-upper: Splash cold water over your face and run wrists under the cold water tap.

Drinking tea? Get added zip by splashing a little sherry (dry, cream or Amontillado) into your piping hot cup.

Another bracing drink can be fixed in a minute: Add a stick of cinnamon to ½ cup of chicken or beef broth and bring to a boil. Add ½ cup of tomato juice and heat well. Pour, with the cinnamon stick, into a mug or soup bowl.

Stretch like a cat to banish tension. Lie on your bed or on the floor and stretch out like a cat, from head to toe. Raise your arms over your head and pull those legs out of their sockets! Reach with your fingertips toward one wall and toward the opposite wall with your toes. Unkink those muscles—tension uses a lot of valuable energy.

Think about a beach at sunset, a mountaintop in the snow, a clear lake—whatever setting makes you tranquil. Keep the picture in your mind by closing your eyes and holding it there. Feel your body relax.

If you feel really tied up in knots, yell! This is one practically sure way of feeling better, only be sure to scream in a spot where family and neighbors won't get alarmed and call the police.

De-tense in the fetal position: Kneel on your knees, sitting on your heels. Stretch your arms in front of you on the floor, with palms down. Now rest your forehead on the floor. Breathe slowly and regularly until you feel calmer.

Use finger pressure to relieve a tension headache. With your fingertips, feel all over your head. When you come to a spot that is sore or extra sensitive to the touch, place your middle finger on it and gently rotate it until the soreness subsides. Go over your entire head this way.

If you own one, use your shower massager on tense parts of the body—your spine, shoulders, thighs or backs of calves. Turn the pressure up and let the water pulsate over knotted muscles. Or try this trick with the pulsating spray of your garden hose nozzle. The tight areas will loosen up.

Do a shoulder stand. Lie down on the floor. Bring your knees to your chest, then straighten them till your legs are pointing up. Raise your hips and support your back with your hands. Hold that position for a few minutes, breathing deeply. Feel the blood rush to your head. Now bend your knees and slowly unroll your back until it and your feet are flat on the floor. Feel more relaxed?

Childhood foods—your all-time, old-time favorites —will sometimes soothe and calm you like nothing else. Ice cream, cookies, spaghetti and butter, hot cereal, peanut butter and jelly, cream of tomato soup . . . the choice is individual, but the trick usually works, taking you back to the security blanket of the past. Use this play only occasionally; childhood foods can also make you fat.

Sip peppermint or spearmint tea. Herbs of the mint family are soothing to the body.

When you feel uptight, take a bath. Add perfume to the tub, bring in a pretty candle and a portable radio tuned to a relaxing music station, and lie back . . . the environment will help banish stress.

Have a container of yogurt. Like milk, yogurt contains calcium, which has a mild sedative effect on the body and makes you feel more relaxed.

Distract your mind when you're under pressure. Do something frivolous, nonstressful and unrelated to "real life." Watch an old movie on TV, play with your dog, do a crossword puzzle, take a long swim or do a few rows on the sweater you're knitting.

Have someone massage your neck and shoulders. Just two or three minutes of work on those tensed-up muscles will loosen you up—and the touch of a human hand will reassure you that somebody cares.

Avoid overeating refined sugar when you're especially nervous. Sugar may pick you up for a few minutes, but you'll experience a quick letdown—possibly ending up even more anxious than you were before. This "hypoglycemic effect" doesn't do you any good right now.

Don't binge when you're under stress. Though it's a temptation to keep stuffing yourself, don't. When you feel better, you'll still be fat.

Stress is stress, but depression is different. If you've been down in the dumps, very tense or confused for more than a week or two, seek professional help. Your doctor or clergyman is someone to whom you might turn. Very often you'll feel better after a talk with one or the other. But if you need it or want it, low-cost mental health services are available in most communities.

Establish a bedtime routine and follow it nightly. A warm bath, a plate of cookies and a glass of milk, easy-listening music . . . repeated rituals, whatever they are, will automatically suggest sleep.

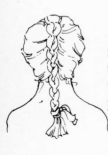

Hair should never pull tightly when you sleep. Hard rollers and metal clips are a bad idea. So is a ponytail. If you have long hair, braid it loosely. Too much tension is painful, making it hard to sleep, and also pulls out your hair.

Snack lightly at bedtime if you are hungry. Drink

a cup of milk and munch two or three crackers. An empty stomach will only prevent easy sleep, since you'll be aware of hunger pangs and possibly be kept up by those gurgling noises.

Sleep in a cool room, not a stuffy, overheated one. Experiments show that sleep is sounder if there is fresh air circulating.

If you are exhausted, don't stay up just to stay up. Many people hate to go to sleep for fear of missing something. The night hours, when you're away from job pressures and children's demands, are definitely to be savored, but not at the expense of the rest your body needs.

Great falling-asleep trick: Close your eyes and picture yourself asleep in a peaceful setting.

Breathe shallowly and slowly, and you will quickly grow drowsy because of decreased oxygen to the brain. Take in only a little bit of air as you inhale.

Count backwards from one hundred on each exhaled breath to fall asleep. Count very slowly—you won't remember getting to one!

Don't sleep on a full stomach. A light snack before bedtime is fine, but a heavy meal will prevent you from sleeping comfortably—your body will be too busy with digestion.

For chronic insomnia, take two calcium tablets with a glass of milk before retiring. Both are natural, safe tranquilizers.

Make your bed more attractive, and you'll be more interested in sleeping in it. Keep sheets and covers fresh. You might also spray once or twice over your sheets with your favorite cologne to make your bed deliciously fragrant.

Avoid exercising just before bedtime. The activity is far too stimulating to permit easy sleep.

Fight insomnia by going to sleep at the same time every night. Keep to the same bedtime hour rigidly for a month, and you should have an easier time falling asleep. Some people, it seems, start to feel more secure with a set bedtime.

If you have insomnia, use the time before you go to bed for routine—but nonstressful—jobs, like doing your manicure, polishing your shoes, cleaning the silver or ironing a blouse. Don't watch violence on TV, and keep away from stimulating books or magazines. A dull but satisfying activity is ideal.

How about a nightlight? If your insomnia stems from the fears of childhood, this may do the trick. It's worth a try.

Go with your biological clock. If you are a "night person" who simply isn't sleepy before midnight, accept the fact. Go to bed later and get up later. If you're on an "early bird" clock, retire earlier in the evening and get up earlier. Trying to go to sleep when you're honestly not ready to is a situation often mistaken for insomnia.

Get in the mood for sleep. Relax your body by lying on the floor with your feet elevated. Rest them on the seat of a chair or sofa.

For insomniacs and anyone with cold feet: Go to bed with a hot-water bottle. The warmth will make you feel cozy—an inducement to sound sleep.

Relax your body, part by part, to fall asleep: Start with the toes. Say to yourself, "My toes are free of tension . . . they're totally relaxed . . . they're getting heavy . . ." Now move up to your ankles: "My ankles feel relaxed and heavy . . ." (Say it very s-l-o-w-l-y.) Now to your calves. Then your knees, thighs, buttocks, pelvis, abdomen, chest, shoulders, arms, hands, fingers, neck, mouth, eyes, head and finally your mind. You should feel totally calm. Don't let any stray thoughts in. Now drift off blissfully. . . .

Go to bed earlier if you feel and look tired. Just an hour extra can really show in your looks. Sometimes it's the simplest solution that's hardest to find.

Get a bed board. If your mattress is old and soft and

you can't afford a new one, place a bedboard (or a plywood sheet cut to size) under your matress. You'll sleep sounder on a firm surface.

Rise slowly in the morning. Avoid bounding out of bed. Even if you feel like a million dollars, get up in a relaxed way. Too fast is shocking to your system—in particular, your circulation, which must readjust itself every morning to your vertical posture.

Throw out an alarming alarm clock. If the ring is loud and strident, you're waking up to instant stress. You shouldn't be bullied out of bed, just reminded that it's time to start your day. Invest in a softer alarm tone or a clock radio which you can set to easy music.

Exercise mildly two hours before bedtime. A few situps or a ten-minute walk may relax your body for sleep. Anything strenuous, like running, is too stimulating and will only rev you up.

Chapter 15

Seasons of Beauty

*Summer and winter set their own beauty require-
ments. With summer's blazing sun comes the need to
protect our sensitive skins and counteract the effects
of heat on the body. Winter's chill winds rob the skin
of precious moisture. To restore it, a woman must
follow special cold-weather routines. Gearing up for
summer or winter means just a few easy changes. Do
make them.*

Summer/Hot Weather

Between 10 A.M. and 2 P.M., the sun's rays are
strongest. Stay out of the sun at "prime time," or use
extreme caution.

Zinc oxide is old-fashioned and *not* colorless, but
it's still one of the best sunblocks around. Especially if
you're fair and need every bit of protection you can
get, use zinc oxide on your nose, lips, ears . . . those
very delicate areas that burn so easily.

Before you sun, apply hair conditioner with sunscreen—hair can burn, too.

Don't shampoo just before sunbathing. You need

the hair's own natural oils for protection, and shampoo removes them as it cleanses.

Check that any medications you are taking are not photosensitive. Some drugs—for instance, tetracycline —do not react well to sunlight, and the effect can cause skin discoloration.

Mix a bit of sunscreen with your foundation on bright summer days—you can burn just walking down a city street! Blend sunscreen and base in the palm of your hand, then apply as usual.

Soothe sunburned skin by saturating cotton pads with ordinary tea and swabbing over the affected areas.

Wear light colors instead of dark shades. Whether they actually help deflect the sun's rays instead of absorbing them is unclear, but psychologically white, beige and pastel shades make you feel cooler.

Don't shave your legs the same day you're swimming in salt water since the salt can irritate the open hair follicles. Shave the night before.

Talcum powder will remove gritty beach sand from your body. Sprinkle the talc all over, then rub gently with a towel. If you don't have time for a shower, this is a good trick.

Hot weather stimulates oil glands and makes skin greasier. Carry oil-blotting cleansing towelettes in your purse, and refresh your skin during the day as needed.

Help your complexion to slough off dead cells of a tan by using a washcloth to cleanse your face. A complexion brush or special abrasive cleansing pad is a good substitute.

Moisturize your skin often to prevent dryness. Carry a mini-size moisturizer in your purse. Lubricate your complexion whenever it feels taut—one of the signs of dryness.

Cool your astringent in the refrigerator. After cleansing, enjoy an invigorating rinse by splashing over the skin.

Switch to an astringent with a lower alcohol content if yours has a high percentage of alcohol. Alcohol removes too much moisture from the skin.

Summer makeup puts the accent on beautiful eyes and lips. When you spend a great deal of time out of doors and have a naturally healthy color, you don't need a heavy foundation.

Even out a fading tan with a foundation that is one shade darker than your normal tint.

To perk up a sallow tan, stick to the rosier shades to offset the yellow undertones. Avoid using blusher or lipstick with an orange base—corals, rusts, apricots and peaches.

In summer, when your skin is naturally oilier, use powder-formulated blusher and eyeshadow. They'll stay on better and longer than creams, which tend to "slide" around.

Warm baths are better for cooling the body than either hot, which raise your temperature, or cold, which are too stimulating.

Heavy scents are cloying in the heat. Switch to a light cologne like one of the citrus or "green" fragrances.

 A small fan fits easily into any purse and comes in handy on hot buses or in rooms without air conditioning. Treat yourself to a pretty design.

Avoid drinking too much alcohol. A tall, cold beer is enticing, but alcohol interferes with your body temperature's ability to stabilize itself and become used to the heat. Plus, it's a diuretic. In extreme heat, when you're already perspiring heavily, alcohol can be dehydrating.

Sprinkle a little salt on your food to replace what you've lost through perspiration.

Don't overexert yourself in the heat. Do your most strenuous work in the cool morning or evening hours. At hot high noon, move slowly and take short breaks whenever you get tired.

You'll feel coolest if you wear clothing that's loose, lightly woven and made of natural fibers like cotton or linen.

Watch for swollen hands and feet, headaches and low blood pressure—symptoms of chronic vasodilation, which is expansion of the blood vessels near the surface of the skin. If these signs occur, call your doctor.

Shut off the air conditioning whenever possible. This artificial cooling, however comfortable, interferes with your body's natural acclimatizing process, making you all the more vulnerable to the heat when you venture outside.

Cool your house naturally. Keep the windows closed and shades drawn during the day and open at night. Consider installing awnings to shield windows from the beating sun. Or how about putting in an attic fan to draw that hot air up and out of the house?

Winter/Cold Weather

Taking a walk in a snowy field? Wear a wide-brimmed hat to protect your face from the winter sun.

Wear sunglasses to protect your eyes from the winter glare. Remember, whenever you squint, you're encouraging wrinkles.

Invest in a richer moisturizer now. Low temperatures and icy winds rob the skin of its natural moisture. You'll want products that do the best possible job of sealing in the skin's natural lubrication.

Treat your skin to warm face cream when it's cold outside. Spoon enough cream for one application—say ½ teaspoon—into a clean baby food jar (the smallest size). Place the jar in a shallow pan of water. Heat over a low flame until the cream is warm to the touch. Rub in gently.

Keep an antichap lipstick in the pocket of your everyday winter coat. You'll be able to reapply often, even if you change handbags.

Add to your collection of green plants. Plants are nature's own humidifiers, adding moisture to the air around them—and that's what you need now.

Do you wash your face with soap? Switch to a cleansing cream which removes less oil from the skin. With oily skin, get a cleanser that's rinsable with water and not tissued off.

Use a moisturizing mask once a week. Some good

natural masks are honey, mashed banana or warm
olive oil.

Take quick showers, less drying to your body than
long tub soaks.

Cleanse your body with a clean, wet washcloth or
a loofah—they'll do the job as well as soap without
leaving your skin dry or flaky.

For your complexion's sake—and your budget's—
keep your winter thermostat below 72° F. Above
that, skin becomes dry and flaky.

To fight winter dryness, invest in a special moisturizing makeup foundation.

Refresh your lipstick often, since it acts as a barrier to the weather and prevents lips from chapping.

Wear cream eyeshadows and blushers. Their moist-
ness will feel better, look better and do better for dry
winter skin.

Eye cream is a must. Buy a special preparation, or
just smooth a little olive oil over your eyes at night
before you go to sleep.

Always add bath oil to your winter tub. Your body

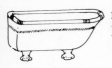

needs softening from the effects of wind and weather. Buy a scented bath oil, or add baby oil to your tub.

Rub body lotion in every day to avoid ugly, cracked skin.

Deep-condition your hair every week with a mayonnaise pack. Comb mayo into your dry hair, wrap your head with plastic wrap and leave on at least one hour. Rinse very well, then shampoo and rinse again.

Massage your scalp every night. At this time of year, you need to stimulate the oil glands more. Massaging also loosens dry flakes that accumulate on the scalp in cold weather.

Rub more conditioner into the ends of your hair. Ends are generally drier than the scalp area, which receives a better supply of oils.

Limit use of your blow-dryer, hot rollers and curling iron. They dry your hair too much. Whenever you can, let your hair dry naturally.

Eat more protein and fat—red meats, eggs, cheese, milk, butter and margarine. Protein and fat take more energy to digest than carbohydrates, so your body stays warmer.

Drink lots of water. Liquids help stabilize your

body temperature and replace the fluids lost through the frequent urination that takes place in cold weather.

Keep up your exercise. Even in the cold months, stay active to stay fit. Switch to indoor tennis or swimming, or change exercises altogether; dance classes and gymnastics are great winter sports.

Wear adequate, protective footwear. Make sure your shoes or boots are insulated and waterproof. Cold, wet feet can lead to frostbite or trench foot— as well as flu.

Cover your feet with baby powder. Talc helps to absorb the perspiration that's inevitable with heavy winter stockings, closed shoes and boots.

Chapter 16

For Mothers-to-Be

Having a baby is a joyous experience which expresses a love shared and a union enriched. Pregnancy has its own beauty, special to this time of a woman's life. Savor this waiting period by paying attention to your changing body, eating healthfully, exercising regularly and treating yourself with lots of tender loving care.

To develop a sense of the beauty of family, fill in the weeks of waiting by framing photographs of all your relatives and hanging them, gallery style, on a wall where your child can get to know those familiar faces. If you'd rather, you can start your "tree" in a scrapbook that you fill with pictures and mementos.

On the first day of each month of your pregnancy, have your picture taken in profile. This visual record will help you appreciate the amazing metamorphosis your body is undergoing.

Keep a journal. Record the days—good and bad—of your pregnancy for you to read later and share with your child in future years. Write down your feelings and thoughts and describe what's happening to your body.

Fill those waiting days with the aroma of fresh-baked bread. Baking your own yeast bread is wonderfully satisfying and calming. And the bonus is that you will utilize the whole wheat flour (rich in vitamin B-6) that is so good for your baby's growing nervous system.

Take lots of naps—especially during the early months when you may feel very tired. When you do, lie down and rest. Sleep as much as you need to.

Fill your house with flowers. A pitcher full of daisies or lilacs will lift your spirits when you feel down.

Go with the languorous "bovine feeling" of pregnancy. It's natural to feel placid and dreamy at this time, so sit back and relax. Use this time for gentle daydreams and pleasurable plans.

Capitalize on the natural glow that pregnancy gives a woman. You may want to forgo foundation makeup now and just highlight your eyes. Let your own radiance shine.

If your complexion looks better than ever, just give it a fine dusting with translucent powder, and off you go!

Experiment with eye shadow. If you've always worn blue, try green. If your usual shade is green, give violet a whirl. Your glowing skin is the perfect back-drop for sparkling eyes.

How about a wash 'n blow-dry cut? You'll be able to shampoo every day and even look great in the hospital without a set.

Switch to a shampoo for oily hair, or wash more often. Most women's hair becomes limp or oily because the scalp may perspire more heavily during pregnancy.

Condition your hair frequently. Hormonal changes can make your hair dry. If you notice this happening, be sure to use a deep-penetrating hair pack once a week.

You might want to switch to a light lemony or woodsy cologne if odors seem stronger at this time. Sometimes heady perfume can aggravate morning nausea.

Rub a small amount of olive oil or coconut oil over your expanding belly twice a day to help prevent stretch marks and itchy skin.

Switch to a soft toothbrush. If your gums are extra-sensitive now, use a brush with very soft bristles to avoid irritating them further.

Make an appointment to have your teeth cleaned. This is always a perk-up—and good for you, of course.

Investigate the natural childbirth classes in your town. Even if you plan to have some kind of anesthesia during delivery, the breathing exercises you'll learn can ease your labor considerably.

Join an exercise class with other mothers-to-be. The joyous camaraderie will spur you to keep up regular exercise throughout pregnancy (making your delivery smoother, many doctors feel). Check local exercise studios—many hold special classes for pregnant women. Or ask your doctor, who may know of classes.

Walking is terrific exercise. During the last month or two of your pregnancy, walk to the local playground often and watch the children playing. Getting used to little ones and their behavior will ease your transition to motherhood.

Buy a pedometer (the kind you strap to your belt), and try to walk at least one mile a day.

If you swim for exercise, you can continue swimming until quite late in your pregnancy, with your doctor's approval, of course. As well as being a great all-over workout, swimming is particularly soothing to your heavy body since it takes all the weight off your feet.

Sign up for a postpartum exercise class. Committing yourself to regular workouts after the baby is born will make it easier to get your body back in shape.

Keep checking your posture. Since your center of gravity has shifted, it's easy to lapse into a swayback stance—one of the commonest causes of backaches. Practice standing with your heels close to a wall. Try to press every vertebra of your spine against the wall. When you step away from the wall, maintain that good posture.

Try doing kitchen work (such as chopping vegetables or washing dishes) sitting down to take the strain off your legs.

Help ease your aching back by sitting properly. Keep your spine straight, and don't let your hips slide forward in the seat. Touch every vertebra to the back of the chair.

A two-minute foot massage is heaven. Indulge yourself every evening. Better yet, get your husband to knead those tired toes, arches and ankles back to life.

Give your feet a perfumed soak. While you're reading, watching TV or sewing at night, treat yourself to a hot foot bath laced with fragrant bubble bath. Buy a big rubber basin just for this purpose (they're inexpensive).

Put your feet up whenever possible. Arrange permanent footstools and ottomans in the rooms you spend the most time in. They can be conventional footrests or ones you make yourself. Cover a chipboard cube with foam rubber and pretty fabric, or set soft pillows on painted cardboard boxes all around the house.

When you get too big to reach your toes, treat yourself to a pedicure once a month.

Don't think of yourself as fat. You're not—you're pregnant. Fretting about your "ruined" figure will rob you of the special joy of pregnancy. And don't use your expanded figure as an excuse to overeat!

Treat yourself to stylish maternity clothes and comfortable, but flattering shoes. Accessorize your outfits with pretty scarves, beads and earrings, too. It's important to maintain pride in your appearance, since neglecting your looks can depress you very quickly.

If you're self-conscious about your protruding bellybutton under certain clothes, tape a bandaid over it.

Wear low-heeled shoes for maximum comfort and safety.

Wear a bra all through pregnancy. The added support will prevent your breasts from losing their shape.

Carry a pretty handkerchief. At times, you may feel very warm and will perspire more than usual. Use an all-cotton square for patting your face dry.

Eat crunchy salads and fresh fruit every day. As well as providing important vitamins and minerals, these also give you the roughage that helps discourage constipation.

Grow mung bean sprouts. Toss them into your nightly salads. They're rich in folacin, which helps protect your unborn baby. (Find directions for growing sprouts on page 145.)

Have one dark green or deep yellow vegetable every day. Here are some good choices: broccoli, carrots, chard, collards, cress, kale, pumpkin, spinach, sweet potatoes, turnip greens and winter squash.

A glass of orange, tomato or grapefruit juice or these raw fruits are excellent choices for fulfilling the requirements of one to two servings daily of vitamin C.

Most doctors advise having a pint of milk every day. If you dislike plain milk, prepare milk puddings or milk soups. Fruit shakes (blending bananas, strawberries, berries or peaches with milk) are also good ways to take your milk.

Stock up on cheddar and swiss cheese if you can't digest milk sugars. Yogurt and buttermilk may be easier substitutes, too, to help you fulfill the recommended two to four daily servings of milk products for the first half of pregnancy and the four daily servings you require in the second half.

For a mid-afternoon snack, have a cup of plain yogurt with fresh fruit. Count it as one of your servings of "milk."

Sip a glass of prune juice at mid-morning. Not only is this a good source of iron, but it will ease the sluggish elimination that so often accompanies pregnancy.

Instant gratification mix: ½ cup sunflower seeds, ½ cup raw peanuts, ½ cup raisins, ½ cup chopped, dried apricots and ¼ cup shredded coconut. Shake together in a plastic bag. Tie and store in a handy place for moments of craving. This healthy blend is super-high in iron.

A hot pick-me-up for working mothers-to-be: A dash of lime juice in a cup of boiling water. Keep an immersion heater, mug and bottle of lime juice in your desk drawer to mix this vitamin C-rich beverage.

Restrict your alcohol intake, since heavy drinking can cause harm to your baby.

You shouldn't take any medications without consulting your obstetrician. Discuss the subject on your visit to the doctor.

When you feel moody (and you *will* feel moody!), don't rely on tranquilizers—they can hurt your baby. Rather, indulge in reading a movie magazine, knitting or bread baking. Any nonintellectual activity can be therapeutic and will help divert your worries.

Sing a song when you feel depressed. Open your mouth and really belt out the words to "Here Comes the Sun," "Oh, What a Beautiful Morning!"—one of your favorites. Even if you can't carry a tune, you'll feel better.

How about quitting smoking? Many medical authorities believe smoking can harm your child. Women who smoke tend to give birth to smaller babies than women who don't, and the risk of a premature delivery is also greater in smokers.

Accept *all* your feelings about having a baby—even the negative ones. Some days you will feel sorry you ever became pregnant. Doubts and anxieties are natural, so don't give yourself extra worry by also feeling guilty.

During the last few weeks, pack your hospital bag. Along with the obvious, include a pretty new soap to make you feel good, a scented massage cream for your back massages (hospital cream can smell medicinal), hot rollers, dry shampoo, pretty ribbons for your hair and a manicure kit with a great new polish.

Buy an inexpensive eye shadow palette box with a dozen or so different colors, and pack it in your hospital bag. Use those long hours between visitors for practicing new color combinations and eye makeup looks.

Use the last few months of pregnancy for little projects around the house. When Baby arrives, there won't be much spare time for repotting plants, sewing kitchen curtains or making Christmas jellies for next year. Do these things to keep occupied while at home.

The last two weeks before delivery will seem endless. Work on a totally engrossing project like needlepoint, crochet, embroidery, knitting, quilting . . . With the baby's layette completed, how about a pretty bedjacket to perk up your hospital stay?

How about mailing out birth announcements from the hospital? Shop for some cute cards and pack them into your hospital bag, along with your address book and postage stamps. This is a fun project that will help the hours go by pleasantly.

Chapter 17

Tips for Travelers

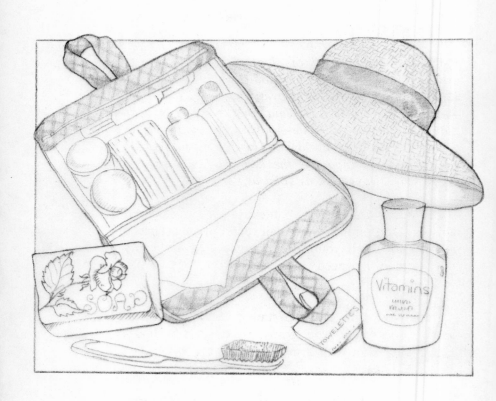

Whether for business or pleasure, it is exciting to travel from one's usual surroundings to a new place. A sense of adventure takes over when we leave home —and it feels wonderful! Beauty on the road is exactly the same as beauty at home—only organized to the nth degree. Paring supplies down to essentials and making your routines compact is the key to a carefree trip where you always look as good as you feel.

Get small-size plastic bottles for your cleanser, moisturizer, shampoo and hair conditioner. There's no need to weigh yourself down with bigger beauty supplies than you need.

Stock your glove compartment with towelettes. Driving does make you grimy, so every few hours cleanse your skin with a moist tissue.

For taking off makeup and mascara while traveling, buy some eye-cleansing pads—much more convenient than bottled oil or remover.

Traveling must: petroleum jelly. You can use it for moisturizer, hand cream and lip gloss.

A trick to prevent spillage: fill plastic bottles only seven-eighths full, then squeeze the air out at the top to form a vacuum.

Divide your moisturizer between a small plastic bottle for your handbag and a bigger bottle for your suitcase. In the car, on a beach or sightseeing in the sun, you'll want the smaller supply for frequent applications.

Buy a double magnifying/regular mirror that snaps closed self-protectively. The last thing you need is shards of broken mirror in your suitcase.

Tuck a bar of your favorite soap in your bag. In some locales, hotel soap is harsh.

Don't forget your vitamins! Pack these and your prescription drugs along with a copy of your prescription in your bag.

Pack a drug kit. Include Band-Aids, antibacterial cream, aspirin, antacid tablets, insect repellent, sunburn cream and tampons. You won't want to start searching for a drugstore in the middle of an outing. Moreover, if you're traveling abroad, these sundries can be expensive.

On any trip, bring an extra pair of eyeglasses or contact lenses—and your prescription.

A lemon friction lotion will give you a refreshing lift at times on your trip when you can't shower.

Keep a freshen-up kit in your purse. In it, put soap, moisturizer, cologne and your makeup. However you travel, you can fix yourself up before you arrive at your destination.

Visit your hairstylist before you leave on your trip. A freshly trimmed hairdo is always quicker to style.

Neutral henna is a super idea for anyone with a hectic itinerary. As well as adding body to your hair, henna coats the hair shaft, so you'll have to shampoo less often.

Try the local beauty products when traveling in a foreign country for business or pleasure. Buy a fragrant bath soap or an exotic bath oil. Don't experiment with skin cleansers, though. Very few countries monitor the manufacture of beauty products as carefully as the United States does—better not to experiment on your face.

Headed for a hot, humid climate? Take your summer makeup—matte foundation, powder blusher and powder shadows. For cold-weather trips, pack creamy makeup formulations to keep skin moist and soft.

In airplane compartments, where the moisture in

the air is practically nil, skin becomes very dry. Apply moisturizer generously before the plane takes off.

Don't get stuck without a shower cap—pack your own. Your cap can always double as a bathing cap in a pinch.

Take along a big towel. Hotels and motels do provide them, but often their towels are skimpy. Plus, you never know when you might want to stop the car for an impromptu swim. In any case, a big beach-type towel makes a light blanket for cool nights driving in the car.

Eye drops can be a lifesaver. Traveling in a car makes eyes dry and itchy, and airplanes are notoriously parching environments. You'll find yourself reaching for your drops more frequently than you do at home.

South-of-the-border tips: Don't drink the local water. Drink bottled water only. And do carry some antidiarrhea medicine and, if possible, an antibiotic from your doctor—just in case.

Be sure to get an adapter for your hot rollers or blow-dryer if you're traveling out of the States. You won't want to be stranded without these beauty helpers.

Wear a big straw hat. Besides blocking the sun from eyes and skin, a floppy hat is salvation when

your hair needs washing—you just tuck it all up inside, clip on a pair of great earrings and you're ready
for anything!

Pack scarves, at least three: one huge square that
you can wear as a shawl, a beach sarong or a blouson
top; one smaller square for tying on your head or
around your neck; and a long rectangle to tie as a
belt, around a straw hat or, again, for your hair.
You'll be able to do more with your trio of scarves if
all the patterns and colors go together.

Perfect for toilet articles, magazines and all the
things you want at hand when you travel are the
new parachute-cloth carry bags. They're lightweight,
snappy looking and inexpensive.

Don't gorge on vacation. By all means, enjoy new
foods and don't count calories, but, on the other
hand, don't go wild. If you come home overweight,
your trip will be memorable for the wrong reason.

Pack a cooler or ice chest for car trips. In it, put
hard cheese, hard-boiled eggs, cold chicken or ham,
fresh raw vegetables, fruit and a quart or two of iced
tea or mineral water. You'll save money and calories
by not patronizing highway eateries.

Can't open your eyes without early morning coffee?
Pack a jar of instant, a plastic mug and an electric
heating coil. You can sip that first cup while you
dress in your motel room.

On a long trip, keep a big thermos of hot coffee or tea on the car seat next to you.

Tuck a jump rope into your suitcase. You can do this aerobic exercise anywhere—indoors or out.

Many hotels and motels feature indoor pools and saunas. Take full advantage of these fitness facilities to exercise and unwind after a day of sightseeing.

To keep from getting achy on the airplane, do knee raises in your seat. Grasp your right knee and pull it up toward your body. Lower it to the floor. Do this about a dozen times. Repeat with your left leg.

Stretch your legs on a long-distance train ride by walking the entire length of the train once or twice.

Hands get stiff when driving. Unkink muscles by clenching and unclenching your fists twenty-five times. Do this each time you stop for a rest or for gas.

Sitting in the car for hours can make your muscles ache. Every hour, pull over to a rest stop, open the car door and hang your body down between your knees. Bounce ten times to stretch your body and release tension.

Don't remove your shoes on the plane. Feet swell

at high altitudes, and you may have a problem getting them back on when it's time to deplane.

If you can avoid it, don't fly when you have a bad cold or sinusitis. The air pressure of the descent can cause severe ear pain and possible hearing loss.

Chew gum when the plane lands. Opening and closing your mouth helps equalize the pressure on your ears.

Alcohol works more quickly at high altitudes. You may want to request a mixer for your drink.

Traveling east? Get more sleep for a week before you depart so your body can "store" some of the hours you'll be losing en route. If you're going west, sleep as usual or get a bit less—you'll be gaining hours.